Barcelona

TRAVELBUG

Barcelona

Edited, designed and produced in 2006 by Automobile Association Developments Limited for Parragon, Queen Street House, 4 Queen Street, Bath BA1 1HE, UK

Published by AA Publishing (a trading name of Automobile Association Developments Limited, whose registered office is Fanum House, Basing View, Basingstoke, Hampshire, RG21 4EA. Registered number 1878835).

ISBN-10: 0-7495-4644-1
ISBN-13: 978-0-7495-4644-1

Material in this book may have appeared in other AA publications.

A CIP catalogue record for this book is available from the British Library.

Printed and bound by Everbest, China

Find out more about AA Publishing and the wide range of services the AA provides by visiting our website at **www**.theAA.com

A02441

Contents

KEY TO SYMBOLS

Throughout the guide a few straightforward symbols are used to denote the following categories:

- address or location
- telephone number
- opening times
- restaurant or café on premises or near by
- nearest underground train station
- nearest bus/tram route
- nearest overground train station
- facilities for visitors with disabilities
- admission charge
- tourist information
- other practical information
- ➤ indicates the page where you will find a fuller description

This book is divided into six sections to cover the most important aspects of your visit to Barcelona.

Our choice of the Top Ten attractions in Barcelona with practical information.

Discover pages 38–197

Two sections: Barcelona and Catalonia, each with brief introductions and a listing of the main attractions

Practical information

6 suggested walks

2 suggested tours

Listings of the best places to eat and stay

Shopping and leisure pages 198–231

Listings of the best places shop, take the children and be entertained.

What you need to know pages 232–249

A practical section containing essential travel information.

Maps

A list of the maps that have been used in this travel guide can be found in the index on pages 250–253.

Prices

Where appropriate, an indication of the cost of an establishment is given by **€** signs:

€€€ denotes higher prices, **€€** denotes average prices, while **€** denotes lower charges.

Barcelona is one of Europe's top destinations. The only problem you will encounter is that there will never be enough time to explore its many museums and monuments, churches and galleries, its fascinating seaboard and, above all, its delectable cuisine.

To enjoy your stay to the full, you will need to adopt the Barcelonan lifestyle – a striking blend of businesslike efficiency combined with long alfresco lunches, lazy siestas, ritual evening promenades and an intoxicating nightlife.

10 Top Tips

If you have only a short time to visit Barcelona and would like to get a really complete picture of the city, here are the essentials:

- **Stroll along La Rambla** (➤ 16), pause for a coffee and listen to the street performers.

- **Get into Gaudí**, especially Casa Milà (➤ 52), Parc Güell (➤ 21) and the famous Sagrada Família (➤ 30).

- **Follow in the footsteps** of Picasso and Dalí and wander at length through the maze of narrow streets in the Barri Gòtic (➤ 55, 60).

- **Enjoy the wide variety** of tapas (➤ 146–153) available in the local bars.

- **Join locals to dance** the *sardana*, the national dance of Catalonia.

- **Experience the tastes**, fragrances and colours of the Mediterranean at Mercat de la Boqueria (➤ 74).

- **Visit Museu Picasso** (➤ 28).

- **Shop for Spanish fashion** and designer gifts in the smart Eixample district (➤ 64, 66).

- **Watch FC Barça play** a home match (➤ 92).

- **Walk the waterfront** (➤ 121) and sample the freshest of seafood.

10 Top Places

La Rambla

Sooner or later, every visitor joins the locals swarming day and night down La Rambla, the most famous walkway in Spain.

This magnificent 18th-century tree-lined walkway, running through the heart of the old city down to the port, is the pride of Barcelona. The central promenade is split into various distinctive sections strung head-to-tail, each with their own history and characteristics, from the flower stalls along Rambla de les Flors to the birdcages of Rambla dels Ocells (Boulevard of the Birds, ➤ 84). And it is said if you drink from the famous fountain (➤ 84) in La Rambla de Canaletes you are sure to return to the city.

Promenading La Rambla is never the same twice, changing with the seasons, by the day and by the hour. It's an experience eagerly shared by people from every walk of life – tourists, locals, bankers, Barça fans, artists, beggars, street-performers, newspaper-sellers, pickpockets, nightclubbers, students, lovers and theatre crowds – all blending together with the noise of the traffic, the birdsong, the buskers, and the scent of the flowers.

Catalunya, Drassanes, Liceu 14, 38, 59, 91 Boat excursions from Moll de les Drassanes) Sant Jordi (St George's Day) celebrations on 23 April (➤ 229). Beware of pickpockets

Catedral

Barcelona's great cathedral is not only one of the most celebrated examples of Catalan Gothic style, but also one of the finest cathedrals in Spain.

The cathedral is located at the heart of the Barri Gòtic (➤ 60–61), on the remains of an early Christian basilica and a Romanesque church. Most of the building was erected between the late 13th century and the middle of the 15th century, although the ornate main façade and octagonal dome were constructed at the beginning of the 20th century.

The impressive interior represents a harmonious blend of medieval and Renaissance styles, with a lofty triple nave, graceful arches, 29 side chapels and an intricately carved choir. Beneath the main altar is the crypt of Santa Eulàlia (the patron saint of Barcelona), which contains her tomb.

Near the main entrance is the Chapel of Christ of Lepanto (formerly the chapter house), which is widely considered to be the finest example of Gothic art in the cathedral. It contains the crucifix carried on board *La Real*, the flagship of Don Juan of Austria (➤ 62), during the famous Battle of Lepanto.

The 14th-century cloister is the most beautiful part of the cathedral, its garden of magnolias, palms and fountains making a cool retreat from the heat of the city. There is even a small pond, with a flock of white geese, supposedly symbolising Santa Eulàlia's virginal purity. A small **museum** just off the cloister shelters many of the cathedral's most precious treasures.

Despite its grandeur, the cathedral remains very much a people's church. Worshippers outnumber tourists and on Sundays Barcelonans gather in Plaça de la Seu at noon to perform the *sardana*, a stately Catalan folk dance which symbolises unity.

✉ Plaça de la Seu 3 ☎ 93 310 71 95 ⌚ Daily 8–1.15, 5–7.30 Ⓜ Jaume I 🚌 17, 19, 40, 45 ✋ Free

Museum

☎ 93 315 22 13

⌚ Daily 10–12.45, 5–6.45

✋ Inexpensive ? Small gift shop

Parc Güell

Deemed a failure in its day, Gaudí's eccentric hilltop park is now considered one of the city's treasures and a unique piece of landscape design.

The architectural work of Gaudí is inseparable from Barcelona, largely thanks to his relationship with the Güells, a family of industrialists who commissioned from him a number of works. For Parc Güell, Don Eusebi Güell, Gaudí's main patron, had grand ideas for a residential English-style garden city, with 60 houses set in formal gardens. Gaudí worked on the project from 1900 to 1914, but it proved an economic disaster: only three houses were completed, and the park became city property in 1923.

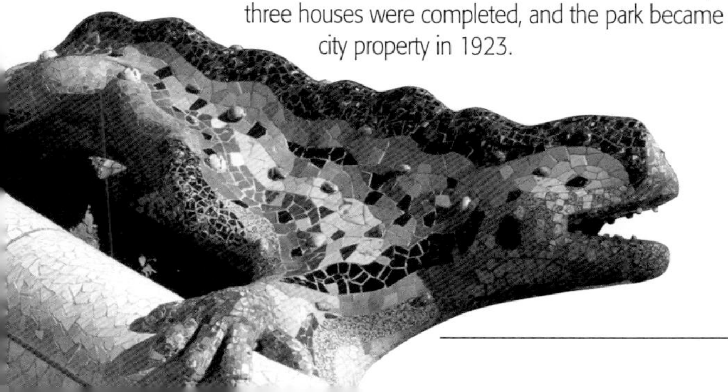

The park's main entrance is marked by two eccentric pavilions. A grand stairway, ornamented by a dragon fountain, leads to a massive cavernous space, originally intended as the marketplace. Its forest of pillars supports a rooftop plaza bordered by a row of curved benches, covered in multicoloured *trencadís* (broken ceramics).

Throughout the 20 hectares of Mediterranean-style parkland, there are sculptures, steps and paths raised on columns of 'dripping' stonework. Gaudí himself lived in one of the houses from 1906 to 1926. Built by his pupil Berenguer, it is now the Casa-Museu Gaudí (☎ 93 219 38 11) and contains models, furniture, drawings and other memorabilia of the architect and his colleagues.

✉ Main entrance: Carrer Olot ☎ 93 213 04 88 🕐 Daily May–Aug 10–9, Sep and Apr 10–8, Oct and Mar 10–7, Nov–Feb 10–6 🍴 Self-service bar Ⓜ Lesseps or Vallcarca (and uphill walk) 🚌 24, 25, 28, 87 ✋ Free

Museu Nacional d'Art de Catalunya (MNAC)

Dominating the northern flank of Montjuïc, this imposing neoclassical palace contains a treasure trove of Catalan art spanning several centuries.

The National Museum of Catalan Art is one of the best museums of medieval art in the world. Housed in an extravagant National Exhibition building, built as the symbol of the 1929 World Exhibition (➤ 36), the museum is currently undergoing renovation by architect Gae Aulenti, who also converted the Gare d'Orsay into one of Paris's foremost museums.

The MNAC boasts the world's most eminent Romanesque art collection, with stone sculptures, wood carvings, gold and silverwork, altar cloths, enamels and coins and a beautifully presented series of 11th- and 12th-century murals, carefully stripped from church walls throughout Catalonia and precisely reconstructed in apses, as if they were still in their original locations. The idea for this collection originated in the early 20th century when the theft of national architectural treasures in Catalonia was at its height, necessitating a church-led crusade to move some of the region's most precious treasures to a safe location.

The museum's Gothic collection forms a striking contrast with more than 400 highly ornate retables and sculptures, including an extraordinary 15th-century Virgin in full flamenco dress. A somewhat fragmented collection of Renaissance and baroque paintings embraces works by Tintoretto, El Greco and Zurbarán.

The museum also contains the Museum of Drawings and Prints, the Numismatic Museum of Catalonia, the Museu d'Art Modern (➤ 85), which moved here from the Ciutadella Park in 2004, and will eventually house the General Library of Art History.

✉ Palau Nacional, Parc de Montjuïc ☎ 93 622 03 76
🕐 Tue–Sat 10–7; Sun and hols 10–2.30. Closed Mon
🍴 Café-bar (€) Ⓜ Espanya 🚌 9, 13, 30, 50, 55 ♿ Excellent
💰 Expensive; free first Thu of month

Montjuïc

Few can resist the charms of the city's local hill, with its museums, galleries, gardens and other attractions set in an oasis of natural calm.

The history of Montjuïc, a 213m hill south of the city and the dominant feature of its coast and skyline, has been linked to the city's history since prehistoric times. It is called 'Mountain of the Jews', after an early Jewish necropolis here. The castle, standing on the bluff, dates from the 16th to 18th centuries and houses the **Museu Militar**, exhibiting collections of military weaponry and uniforms from different countries and periods.

In 1929 Montjuic was the venue for the International Expo and today many of its buildings are filled with museums. The **Museu Arqueològic** and the **Museu Etnològic** typify the Expo's architecture, as does the Palau Nacional, home of the Museu Nacional d'Art de Catalunya (➤ 25).

Beneath the Palau Nacional, Plaça d'Espanya marks the main entrance to the Expo with Venetian towers, and an avenue leading to Plaça de la Font Màgica a spectacular sight that always draws the crowds. The road continues up past the Pavello Barcelona and the Poble Espanyol (➤ 36) to

Fundació Joan Miró (➤ 32) and the Anella Olímpica (➤ 44), venue for much of the 1992 Olympic Games.

Cafés and restaurants (€–€€) Espanya 50, 51 Montjuïc funicular from Paral.lel Metro Free

Museums

Museu Militar: 93 329 86 13: Museu Arqueològic: 93 424 65 77; Museu Etnològic: 93 424 64 02 Tue–Sun, times vary

Inexpensive; Museo Etnològic free first Sun of month

Museu Picasso

This fascinating museum traces the career of the most acclaimed artist of modern times, from early childhood sketches to the major works of later years.

The Picasso Museum is the city's biggest tourist attraction. It contains one of the world's most important collections of Picasso's work and until 2003, when the impressive Museo Picasso Málaga opened in his birthplace, was the only one of significance in his native country.

Pablo Ruiz Picasso was born in Andalucia, but moved to the Catalan capital in 1895, aged 14. He was an exceptionally gifted artist and, by the time of his first exhibition in 1900, was well known. In 1904 he moved to Paris, but remained in contact with Barcelona.

The museum contains work from his early years, notably a series of impressionistic landscapes and seascapes, a portrait of his aunt, Tía Pepa (1896), notebook sketches and paintings of street scenes,

including *Sortida del Teatre* (1896) and *La Barceloneta* (1897), and the menu for *Els Quatre Gats* (Four Cats) café (➤ 135). Other works are from the Blue Period (1901–1904), the Pink Period (1904–1906), the Cubist (1907–20) and neoclassical (1920–25) periods, through to the mature works of later years. There are also 41 ceramic pieces donated by his wife, Jacqueline in 1982, which graphically demonstrate Picasso's astonishing artistic development.

Carrer Montcada 15–23 93 319 63 10 Tue–Sat and hols 10–8, Sun 10–3. Closed Mon Café-restaurant (€€) Jaume I 14, 17, 19, 36, 39, 40 45, 51, 57, 59, 64, 157 Very good Expensive (free first Sun of month)

La Sagrada Família

Big Ben, the Eiffel Tower…most cities have a distinctive monument. Barcelona has Gaudí's Sagrada Família, his, as yet unfinished, cathedral.

Antoni Gaudí, the internationally prestigious figure of Catalan architecture, started work on La Sagrada Família (Temple of the Holy Family) in 1882, and for the latter part of his life dedicated himself entirely to his great vision for Europe's biggest cathedral. His dream was to include three façades representing the birth, death and resurrection of Christ, and 18 mosaic-clad towers symbolising the Twelve Apostles, the four Evangelists, the Virgin Mary, and Christ. On Gaudí's untimely death in 1926, only the crypt, one of the towers, the majority of the east (Nativity) façade, and the apse were completed. Ever since, the fate of the building has been the subject of often bitter debate.

With a further estimated 80 years of work (which would include the destruction of several buildings in Carrer Mallorca and Carrer Valencia), it seems that the Sagrada Família will probably never be more than a shell. Even as it stands today, it has become a world-wide symbol of Barcelona and one of the great architectural wonders of the world.

✉ Plaça Sagrada Família ☎ 93 207 30 31 🕓 Daily Apr–Sep 9–8, Oct–Mar 9–6 Ⓜ Sagrada Família 🚌 19, 33, 34, 43, 44, 50, 51, 54 ♿ Few 💰 Expensive (additional charge for lift) ❓ Crypt museum, gift shop, lift and stairway to the towers

Fundació Joan Miró

This dazzling gallery pays homage to Joan Miró, one of Catalonia's greatest artists, famous for his childlike style and use of vibrant colours.

The Miró Foundation was set up by Joan Miró in 1971, and is devoted to the study of his works and to the promotion of all contemporary art. The gallery is itself a masterpiece and a perfect place in which to pursue the foundation's aims. It contains some 200 Mirónian paintings, 153 sculptures, 9 tapestries, his complete graphic works and over 5,000 drawings, making it one of the world's most complete collections of this great master.

Miró was born in Barcelona in 1893 and, apart from a brief spell in Paris, spent most of his life in the city developing his bold style of vigorous lines and primary colours. In 1956 he moved to Mallorca where he died in 1983.

Highlights of the gallery include some of Miró's earliest sketches, the tapestry *Tapis de la Fundació* and a set of black-and-white lithographs entitled *Barcelona Series* (1939–44) – an artistic appraisal of the war years.

✉ Avinguda de Miramar, Parc de Montjuïc ☎ 93 443 94 70 Oct–Jun Tue–Sat 10–7, Thu till 9.30; Jul–Sep Tue–Sat 10–8, Thu till 9.30; Sun & hols 10–2.30 Café-restaurant (€€) Espanya 50, 55 Good Expensive

Santa Maria del Mar

Barcelona's seaside cathedral is a Gothic triumph, built to demonstrate Catalan supremacy in Mediterranean commerce.

The 14th-century church of Santa Maria del Mar (St Mary of the Sea) is located at the heart of La Ribera (Waterfront), the medieval city's maritime and trading district.

The church was built between 1329 and 1384 and has a purity of style that makes it one of the finest examples of Barcelona's Gothic heritage. The plain exterior is characterised by horizontal lines and two octagonal, flat-roofed towers. Inside, the wide, soaring nave and high, narrow aisles, all supported by slim, octagonal columns, provide a great sense of spaciousness. The ornaments of the side chapels were lost when the city was besieged by Bourbon troops in 1714 and during the Spanish Civil War. The resulting bareness of the interior, apart from the sculpture of a 15th-century ship that sits atop the altar, helps you to admire the church's simplicity without distraction.

✉ Plaça de Santa Maria ☎ 93 310 23 90 🕒 Daily 9–1.30, 4.30–8 (from 10am Sun) Ⓜ Barceloneta, Jaume I 🚌 14, 17, 36, 39, 40, 45, 51, 57, 59, 64, 157 ♿ Good ✋ Free

Poble Espanyol

You can tour the whole of Spain in an afternoon here at Barcelona's 'Spanish Village', a remarkable showcase of regional architectural styles.

Built for the 1929 World Exhibition, the Poble Espanyol (Spanish Village) was intended as a re-creation of the diversity of Spanish regional architecture through the ages. It could easily have resembled a stage set or a theme park, but instead, the 115 life-sized reproductions of buildings, clustered around six squares and 3km of streets, form an authentic village, where visitors can identify famous or characteristic buildings ranging from the patios of Andalucia to Mallorcan mansions and the granite façades of Galicia.

Within the village are bars and restaurants serving regional specialities, and more than 60 shops selling folk crafts and regional artefacts. Some are undeniably over-priced, but there are also some real finds.

The Museum of Popular Arts, Industries and Traditions and the Museum of Graphic Arts are also located here and

every Sunday at midday, a *festa* enlivens the main square.

The Poble Espanyol was smartened up for the 1992 Olympics, with the introduction of 'The Barcelona Experience' (a half-hour audio-visual history of the city) and several restaurants and bars, including the extraordinary Torres de Ávila (➤ 221), a trendy 'designer bar'-cum-nightclub, one of Barcelona's hottest night spots. Excellent flamenco shows can also be seen at El Tablao de Carmen (➤ 223).

✉ Avinguda de Marqués de Comillas s/n
☎ 93 508 63 30
🕐 Mon 9am–8pm; Tue–Thu 9am–2am; Fri & Sat 9am–4am; Sun 9am–noon
🍴 Plenty (€–€€) 🚇 Espanya
🚌 13, 50 ♿ Only partially accessible to wheelchair users, who have free entry
✋ Expensive

Barcelona 40–127

Where to eat and drink 128–153

Where to stay 154–161

Barcelona

Ever since it was founded more than 2,000 years ago, Barcelona has been striving to become a great metropolis. To its inhabitants, it is not Spain's second city but the capital of Catalonia; not a Spanish metropolis but a European one, and the Spanish leader in both haute couture and haute cuisine. The best time to see Barcelona in its true colours is after FC Barça wins an important match: the streets erupt to the sound of car horns and popping champagne corks.

Visitors to Barcelona, on the other hand, are entranced by the Mediterranean atmosphere of the city, the richness of its art and architectural treasures both ancient and modern, the proud but not narrowly nationalistic character of the people, the strong tradition of theatre and music and the exuberant nightlife. In this dynamic and passionate city, it is easy to live life to the full, both day and night.

MONTANA RUS

THE CITY OF BARCELONA

Barcelona is easy to get to know. It is a compact city, small enough to explore on foot but great enough to be enormously varied. Most of the main sights are in three main areas: the Ciutat Vella (Old City), the Eixample and the Waterfront.

It is easy to lose yourself in the hidden corners of the Old City, to stumble upon a market in a fountain-splashed square, or to write your postcards in the geese-filled cloisters of the cathedral. The Eixample is particularly remarkable for the way the great turn-of-the-19th-century Modernists (*Modernistas*) created some of the most imaginative and bizarre buildings in the world within the confines of a rigid grid system of streets.

The extension of the seafront began with the naming of Barcelona as host city for the 1992 Olympics. Today, with its smart promenades, sandy beaches, and open-air bars and restaurants, Barcelona's image is 'Cara al Mar' ('Face to the Sea'). Leading from the seafront, La Rambla is a bustling avenue of cafés, bookstalls and flower kiosks. By contrast, twin hills Montjuïc and Tibidabo provide panoramic views to the Pyrenean mountains and the sparkling Mediterranean sea.

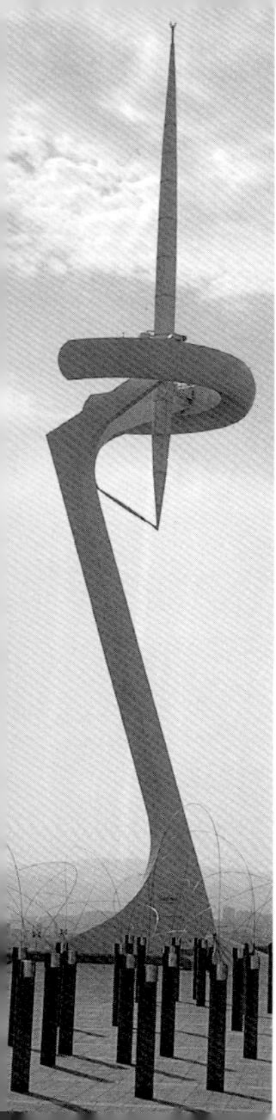

DISCOVER BARCELONA

L'ANELLA OLÍMPICA

In 1992, Montjuïc mountain (➤ 26) became Barcelona's main venue for the Olympic Games. Atop its western crest lies the Anella Olímpica (Olympic Ring), a monumental complex of concrete and marble that contains some of the city's most celebrated new buildings: the Complex Esportiu Bernat Picornell swimming-pool complex; Santiago Calatrava's space-age communications tower, which dominates the skyline; and the remarkable black steel and glass domed Palau de Sant Jordi, designed by Japanese architect Arata Isozaki. Highlights of the games can be relived through video clippings in the Galería Olímpica, located beneath the stadium.

✉ Avinguda de l'Estadi/Passeig Olímpic, Montjuïc ☎ Estadi Olímpic: 93 426 20 89; Palau Sant Jordi: 93 426 20 89; Picornell swimming pools: 93 423 4041 Ⓜ Espanya, or Paral.lel, then Funicular de Montjuïc 🚌 61 ♿ Very good ✋ Free

LA BARCELONETA AND PORT OLÍMPIC

Following the siege and conquest of Barcelona by Felipe V in 1714, a large area of the Ribera district was destroyed to make way for a new citadel. The displaced residents lived for years in makeshift shelters on the beach, until in 1755 a new district was developed on a triangular wedge of reclaimed land between the harbour and the sea, named La Barceloneta (Little Barcelona).

In the 19th century, La Barceloneta became home to seamen and dockers and it is still very much a working district, retaining its distinctive shanty-town atmosphere, fishy smells, and a quayside lined with the boats and nets of the local fleet.

Today most visitors come to La Barceloneta to eat in the many fine seafood eateries (*chiringuitos*), in particular those along the main harbourside thoroughfare, Passeig Joan de Borbó, and the restaurants of the converted Palau de Mar warehouse (➤ 96).

By contrast, Port Olímpic, with its smart promenades and glittering new marina, has given new impetus to Barcelona's nautical activities. Its chic restaurants, cafés and bars have become lively night spots for both locals and tourists. Spain's two tallest buildings preside over the port – the office-filled Torre Mapfre and the five-star hotel Arts Barcelona, Barcelona's top hotel (➤ 154). Near by, a striking bronze fish sculpture (➤ 123) by Frank Gehry (architect of the Guggenheim Museum in Bilbao) heralds the start of the Passeig Marítim, which links the port with La Barceloneta and extends 8km to Sant Adrià del Besòs.

✉ Barceloneta/Port Olímpic 🍴 Plenty (€–€€€) Ⓜ Barceloneta, Ciutadella/Vila Olímpica, Diagonal Mar 🚌 Barceloneta: 17, 36, 39, 40, 45, 57, 59, 64, 157. Port Olímpic: 10, 45, 57, 59, 71, 92, 157

Stratus
women'secret

CASA AMATLLER

Chocolate manufacturer Antonio Amatller i Costa commissioned Josep Puig i Cadafalch to remodel Casa Amatller into an extravagant home with a neo-Gothic façade decorated with sculptures, coats of arms and floral reliefs, and crowned by a stepped gable. Note the beautiful wooden lift and the amazing carvings on one interior doorway depicting animals making chocolate. A combined ticket is available for a guided tour, *La Ruta del Modernisme*, which includes the three façades of Casa Amatller, Casa Batlló and Casa Lleó-Morera and discounted entry to attractions.

✉ Passeig de Gràcia 41 ☎ 93 488 01 39 ⌚ Mon–Sat 10–7, Sun 10–2 🚇 Passeig de Gràcia ♿ Good ✋ Free ? The entrance hall, open to the public, contains the information centre for *La Ruta del Modernisme*

CASA BATLLÓ

Casa Batlló is one of the most famous buildings of the *Modernista* school, designed by Gaudí for Josep Batlló i Casanovas and completed in 1907. It is said to illustrate the triumph of Sant Jordi (St George) over the dragon (left), with its mosaic façade, covered in glazed blue, green and ochre ceramics, representing the scaly skin of the dragon, its knobbly roof the dragon's back, the tower the saint's cross, and the wave-like balconies the skulls and bones of victims.

✉ Passeig de Gràcia 43 ☎ 93 488 06 66/93 488 30 90 🕐 Daily 9–8; ticket office 9–1.30 🚇 Passeig de Gràcia ♿ Good 💶 Expensive

CASA MILÀ

Known locally as La Pedrera (the quarry), Spain's most controversial apartment block and Antoni Gaudí's last and most famous secular building was built between 1906 and 1912 and shows this great Catalan architect at his most inventive. It also demonstrates Gaudí's genius as a structural engineer, with seven storeys built entirely on columns and arches, supposedly without a single straight line or right-angled corner. Its most distinctive features are the rippling limestone façade, with its intricate ironwork, and the strangely shaped chimneys of the roof terrace.

After years of neglect, Casa Milà was declared a World Heritage Site by UNESCO in 1984, and purchased by the Caixa Catalunya Foundation, which invested over 8,000 million pesetas to restore it to its original glory.

✉ Carrer Provenca 261–265 ☎ 93 484 59 00 🕐 Daily 10–7.30. Guided tours: Mon–Fri at 5.30 in English and Catalan and at 6.30 in Spanish 🚇 Diagonal ♿ Good (but not on roof); excellent toilet ✋ Expensive ? Audio guide available

CASA LLEÓ-MORERA

This striking *Modernista* building is considered Lluís Domènech i Montaner's most exuberant decorative work. Its flamboyant façade cleverly minimises the corner by placing emphasis on ornate circular balconies, columned galleries and oriel windows. Inside, a florid pink mosaic vestibule and open staircase lead to first-floor living quarters, lavishly decorated with stencilled stuccowork, stained glass, marquetry and mosaics, portraying roses, lions and mulberry bushes. It is closed to the public.

✉ Passeig de Gràcia 35 ☎ No phone 🕐 Interior currently not open to the public Ⓜ Passeig de Gràcia

CATEDRAL (➤ 18–20)

CIUTAT VELLA

The tightly packed maze of narrow streets and alleyways of Barcelona's Ciutat Vella (Old City), bordered by the Ramblas, the Ciutadella Park, Plaça Catalunya and the sea, was once enclosed by medieval city walls and, until the massive building boom of the Eixample (➤ 42–43), 150 years ago, comprised the entire city.

At its heart is the Barri Gòtic (Gothic Quarter), one of several clearly identifiable *barris* or districts which make up the Old City. Its roots can be traced back to 15BC, when Roman soldiers established a small settlement called Barcino on a slight hill here called Mons Taber. This remarkable cluster of dark, twisting streets, quiet patios, sun-splashed squares and grand Gothic buildings was built inside the Roman fortifications, at a time when Barcelona, along with Genoa and Venice, was one of the three most important merchant cities in the Mediterranean and possessed untold riches. Its crowning glory, the Catedral (➤ 18), is surrounded by former residences of the counts of Barcelona and the Kings of Catalonia and

Aragón. To the northwest lies Carrer Portaferrissa, the Old City's principal shopping street, with trendy boutiques and shopping arcades. To the south lies the spacious Plaça Sant Jaume (➤ 120) and a cobweb of narrow streets and interconnecting squares, including Plaça Sant Felip Neri, with its fine baroque church, Plaça del Pi, with its market of local produce, and leafy Plaça Sant Josep Oriol, the 'Montmartre of Barcelona', where local artists display their works at weekends and buskers entertain the café crowds. Just off the square, the narrow streets bounded by Carrer Banys Nous, Call and Bisbe once housed a rich Jewish ghetto called *El Call*, but now the area is known for its antique shops.

As the city grew more prosperous in the early Middle Ages, new *barris* developed around the Roman perimeter, including La Mercè to the south and La Ribera to the east. The area south of Carrer de Ferran – La Mercè – is focused around the elegant, arcaded Plaça Reial (➤ 118) and the Church of La Mercè, Barcelona's patron Virgin. Though once very prosperous, this *barri* has become shabby and run-down, but is still worth exploring if only to seek out the excellent locals' *tapas* bars along Carrer de la Mercè.

The *barri* of La Ribera, east of Via Laietana, holds much to interest the visitor. Its name (Waterfront) recalls the time when the shoreline reached considerably farther inland during Barcelona's Golden Age, when it was the city's main centre of commerce and trade and the favourite residential area of the merchant élite. Their handsome Gothic palaces still line its main street, Carrer Montcada. Several have since been converted into museums and galleries including Museu Picasso (➤ 28–29) and Galeria Maeght (➤ 207). The street leads to Santa Maria del Mar, the 'seaside cathedral' (➤ 34–35) and the Passeig del Born, with its popular restaurants, bars and craft shops.

Plenty (€–€€€) Jaume I, Liceu, Plaça de Catalunya, Urquinaona

CENTRAL BARCELONA
0
300
600 m
0
300
600 yards
PLAÇA DE JOAN CARLES I
Museu de la Música
Conservatori Municipal de Música
Sargada Família
Mercat de la Concepció
Palau Montana
Casa Milà
Fundació Antoni Tàpies
Església de la Concepció
CARRER D'ARAGO
PLAÇA DE TETUAN
CATALANES
GRAN VIA DE LES CORTS
RAMBLA DE CATALUNYA
PASSEIG DE GRACIA
Casa Batlló
Casa Amatller
CARRER DE BALMES
Casa Lleo - Morera
Manzana de la Discòrdia
RONDA DE SANT PERE
Universitat
RONDA UNIVERSITAT
PLAÇA DE CATALUNYA
CARRER DE PELAI
Sant Pere
Palau de la Música
Arc de Triomf
PASSEIG DE CARLES I
Museu de Zoologia
Parc de la Ciutadella
Museu d'Art Modern
Museu de Geologia
Parc Zoològic
VIA LAIETANA
Museu Picasso
Santa Maria del Mar
Estació Barcelona Terme-França
RONDA LITORAL
CIUTAT VELLA
Catedral
Església de Betlem
Palau de la Virreina
Palau de la Generalitat
Museu d'Història de la Ciutat
PASSEIG ISABEL II
Ajuntament
Museu d'Art Contemporani de Barcelona
RONDA DE SANT ANTONI
LA RAMBLA
PLAÇA D'ANTONI LOPEZ
LA BARCELONETA
Hospital de la Santa Creu i Sant Pau
Gran Teatre del Liceu
PLAÇA REIAL
Moll del Dipòsit
Moll d'Espanya
Palau de Mar
Museu de Cera
PASSEIG DE COLOM
RONDA DE SANT PAU
Palau Güell
Monument a Colom
Moll de la Fusta
Port Vell
IMAX
Aquàrium
Maremagnum
Playa de la Barceloneta
Drassanes & Museu Marítim
AVINGUDA DEL PARAL-LEL
Sants Montjuic
M

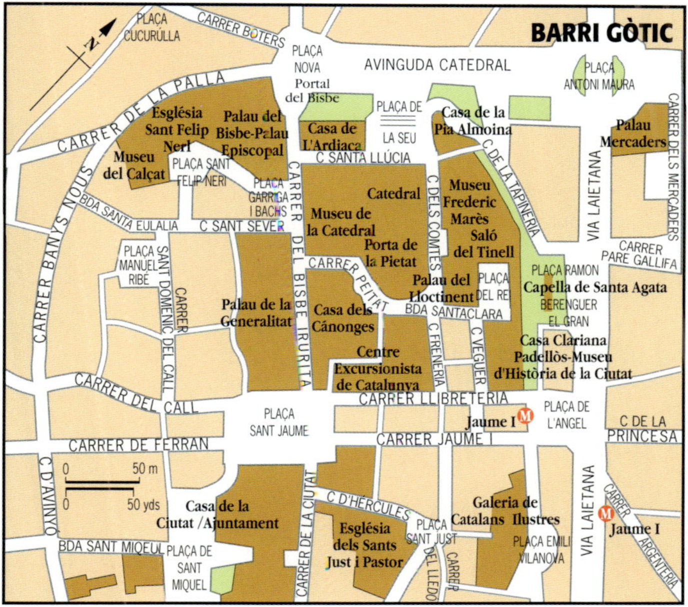
BARRI GÒTIC
N
PLAÇA CUCURULLA
CARRER BOTERS
PLAÇA NOVA
Portal del Bisbe
AVINGUDA CATEDRAL
PLAÇA ANTONI MAURA
CARRER DE LA PALLA
Església Sant Felip Neri
Palau del Bisbe-Palau Episcopal
Casa de L'Ardiaca
PLAÇA DE LA SEU
Casa de la Pia Almoina
Palau Mercaders
CARRER DELS MERCADERS
Museu del Calçat
PLAÇA SANT FELIP NERI
PLAÇA GARRIGA I BACHS
C SANTA LLÚCIA
C DE LA TAPINERIA
VIA LAIETANA
CARRER BANYS NOUS
BDA SANTA EULALIA
C SANT SEVER
CARRER DEL BISBE IRURITA
Catedral
Museu de la Catedral
Porta de la Pietat
C DELS COMTES
Museu Frederic Marès
Saló del Tinell
CARRER PARE GALLIFA
PLAÇA MANUEL RIBÉ
SANT DOMENIC DEL CALL
CARRER
CARRER PEITAT
Palau del Lloctinent
PLAÇA DEL REI
PLAÇA RAMON BERENGUER EL GRAN
Capella de Santa Agata
Palau de la Generalitat
Casa dels Cànonges
BDA SANTACLARA
C FRENERIA
C VEGUER
Casa Clariana Padellòs-Museu d'Història de la Ciutat
Centre Excursionista de Catalunya
CARRER DEL CALL
CARRER LLIBRETERIA
PLAÇA SANT JAUME
Jaume I
PLAÇA DE L'ANGEL
C DE LA PRINCESA
CARRER DE FERRAN
CARRER JAUME I
C D'AVINYO
0
50 m
0
50 yds
Casa de la Ciutat / Ajuntament
CARRER DE LA CIUTAT
C D'HÈRCULES
Església dels Sants Just i Pastor
PLAÇA SANT JUST
Galeria de Catalans Ilustres
PLAÇA EMILI VILANOVA
VIA LAIETANA
CARRER ARGENTERIA
Jaume I
BDA SANT MIQUEL
PLAÇA DE SANT MIQUEL
DEL LLEDÓ
CARRER

walk

Leave Plaça Nova via the Portal del Bisbe (part of the Roman wall) into Carrer del Bisbe. Turn first left into Carrer de Santa Llúcia.

Note the tiny chapel of Santa Llúcia to your right, and the Gothic Archdeacon's House (Casa de l'Ardiaca) to your left. Just beyond is the main entrance to the Catedral (➤ 18).

From Plaça de la Seu, follow Carrer dels Comtes beside the cathedral, past Museu Frederic Marès (➤ 89). A left turn into Baixada de Santa Clara leads to Plaça del Rei (➤ 116). Return to the cathedral and skirt round its buttresses past the 14th-century Canon's House (Casa del Cánonges).

Stone plaques on the façade portray twin towers supported by winged goats with lions' feet, the heraldic symbols of medieval Barcelona.

Turn sharp left, then left again onto Carrer del Bisbe, under a bridge and into Plaça Sant Jaume (➤ 120). Take Carrer de la Ciutat, then the first left until you reach Plaça Sant Just.

Here, the Església dels Sants Just i Pastor is reputedly the oldest church in Barcelona. Opposite, note the faded frescos on an elegant townhouse.

Leave the square along Carrer del Lledó. Turn first left then left again at the House of the Blue Tiles. Following the line of the Roman wall, cross Carrer Jaume I and continue up Carrer de la Tapineria, once the main street of medieval shoemakers.

Constructed between 270 and 310 AD, Barcelona's Roman walls were outgrown by the 11th century.

Continue along Carrer de la Tapineria past more Roman remains and return to Plaça Nova.

Distance 2km **Time** 1 hour (excluding visits)
Start/end point Plaça Nova Catalunya, Urquinaona
Coffee break Mesón del Café (€) Carrer Llibreteria 16, just off Plaça Sant Jaume I 93 315 07 54

DRASSANES AND MUSEU MARÍTIM

Barcelona's Museu Marítim (Maritime Museum) is located in the magnificent Drassanes Reials (Royal Shipyards), a splendid example of Gothic civil architecture. Since the 13th century, these impressive yards have been dedicated to the construction of ships for the crowns of Catalonia and Aragon.

Today, their vast, cathedral-like, stone-vaulted halls contain maps, charts, paintings, pleasure craft and other seafaring memorabilia chronicling the maritime history of Barcelona. The most impressive exhibit is a 60m replica of *La Real*, flagship of Don Juan of Austria, which forms part of an exciting 45-minute spectacle – 'The Great Sea Adventure'. Through headphones, visual and acoustic effects, visitors can experience life as a galley slave, encounter a Caribbean storm and join emigrants bound for the New World.

✉ Avinguda de les Drassanes s/n ☎ 93 342 99 20 🕐 Daily 10–7 🍴 Café-restaurant (€) 🚇 Drassanes 🚌 14, 18, 36, 38, 57, 59, 64, 91 ♿ Few 💰 Expensive (free first Sat of each month after 3pm) ❓ Library, bookshop, gift shop

L'EIXAMPLE

L'Eixample means 'The Extension' in Catalan, and this district was laid out between 1860 and 1920 to expand the city beyond the confines of its medieval walls and to link it with the outlying municipalities of Sants, Sarrià-Sant Gervasi and Gràcia.

The innovative plan, drawn up by liberal-minded civil engineer Ildefons Cerdà, broke completely with the tradition of Spanish urban planning, with its geometric grid of streets

running parallel to the seafront, neatly dividing an area of 9sq km into 550 symmetrical blocks. The aptly named Avinguda Diagonal cuts through the rectilinear blocks at 45 degrees to add a touch of originality. The utopian features of Cerdà's plan – such as gardens in the middle of each block and buildings on only two sides – have been largely forgotten, and today many people scorn the district for its monotony while others praise it as a visionary example of urban planning.

The Eixample is divided into two *barris*, either side of Carrer Balmes. *L'Esquerra* (the Left) is largely residential and of less interest to visitors, whereas *La Dreta* (the Right) contains many of Barcelona's greatest *Modernistame* landmarks, including Casa Milà, the three properties of La Manzana de la Discòrdia, the Fundació Antoni Tàpies, the Hospital de la Santa Creu i Sant Pau, and the Sagrada Família. It is also a district of offices, banks and hotels. Chic boutiques and shops line its streets and, at night, Barcelona's smart set frequents its many restaurants, designer bars and discos.

Plenty (€–€€€) Catalunya, Diagonal, Entença, Girona, Hospital Clinic, Passeig de Gràcia, Provença, Tetuan, Vergaguer, Universitat

walk

This walk explores some of Barcelona's lesser-known examples of *Modernista* architecture.

Start in Plaça de Catalunya, and walk up Passeig de Gràcia.

This elegant avenue has its original wrought-iron street lamps with ceramic mosaic seats dating from 1906. Note Nos 6–14 (one of the last *Modernista* constructions), No 18 (the only surviving example of rationalist commercial architecture in Barcelona) and No 21.

Turn left at Casa Lleó-Morera (► 53), along Carrer Consell de Cent then first left into Rambla de Catalunya, past several contrasting Modernista buildings (Nos 47, 54 and 77) until Diagonal. Turn right past Gaudí-influenced Casa Comalat at No 442 by Salvador Valery and continue until Puigi Cadafalch's Palau Quadras at No 373.

This striking neo-Gothic building contains the Museu de la Música. Near by, UNESCO-listed Casa Terrades (Nos 416–20)

is sometimes known as Casa de les Punxes ('House of Spikes') because of its steep gables and red-tiled turrets.

Turn right into Carrer Roger de Lluria, past Palau Montaner (Carrer Mallorca 278), an early work by Domènech i Montaner, and turn left into Carrer València, past Nos 285, 293, and 312, striking Modernista buildings, and a large enclosed market. At Avinguda Diagonal, turn right.

Don't miss the extraordinary undulating wooden façade of Casa Planells (No 332), by one of Gaudí's early collaborators, Josep Maria Jujol.

Turn left into Carrer Sicilia and continue on to the Sagrada Família (➤ 30–31).

Distance 4km **Time** 2–2.5 hours (excluding visits)
Start point Plaça de Catalunya Ⓜ Catalunya **End point** Sagrada Família Ⓜ Sagrada Família **Lunch break** Buy a picnic in the large, covered market (Mercat de la Concepció) to eat in Plaça Sagrada Família. ✉ Mercat de la Concepció, Carrer València

FUNDACIÓ ANTONI TÀPIES

The Tàpies Foundation was begun by Catalan artist Antoni Tàpies in 1984 to promote the study and understanding of modern art. It is housed in the former Montaner i Simon publishing house, built by Lluis Domènech i Montaner between 1880 and 1889, an unusual building that is considered the initiator of the Modernist movement. The striking *Mudejar*-style façade is crowned by an eye-catching tangle of wire and tubing by Tàpies, entitled *Cloud* and *Chair* (1990). Inside, there is an exhaustive library documenting art and artists of the 20th century, and one of the most complete collections of Tàpies' own works.

✉ Carrer d'Aragó 255 ☎ 93 487 03 15 🕐 Tue–Sun 10–8. Closed Mon 🚌 7, 16, 17, 20, 22, 24, 28, 43, 44 🚇 Passeig de Gràcia ♿ Good ✋ Moderate, children under 16 free ? Library and small bookshop

FUNDACIÓ JOAN MIRÓ (➤ 32–33)

GRÀCIA

In 1820, Gràcia was a mere village of about 2,500 inhabitants. By 1897, the population had swollen to 61,000, making it the ninth-largest city in Spain, known as a radical centre of Catalanism and anarchism, still reflected in some street names – Mercat de la Llibertat and Plaça de la Revolució. Since then, Gràcia has been engulfed by the expanding metropolis, yet even now it maintains a village-like, no-frills, bohemian atmosphere and the *Graciencs* still call the cityfolk *Barcelonins*.

There are no real 'tourist' attractions here, except Gaudí's first major commission, Casa Vicens (✉ Carrer de les Carolines 24). Gràcia's real appeal is its muddle of narrow atmospheric streets and squares, and a concentration of reasonably priced bars, restaurants and popular night venues.

🍴 Plenty (€–€€€) 🚇 Fontana, Gràcia, Joanic, Plaça Molina ❓ Festa Major every August (➤ 231)

HOSPITAL DE LA SANTA CREU I SANT PAU

This remarkable hospital complex is a masterpiece of *Modernisme* by innovative architect Lluís Domènech i Montaner. Not only did he deliberately defy the orderliness of the Eixample by aligning the buildings at 45 degrees to the street grid, but he also built the complex in contradiction to established hospital concepts by creating a 'hospital-village' of 48 small pavilions connected by underground passages and surrounded by gardens, rather than one single massive building.

Construction began in 1902, as a long-overdue replacement for the old hospital in the Raval, following a bequest from a Catalan banker called Pau Gil. The new hospital was inaugurated in 1930. The main pavilion, with its graceful tower and ornate mosaic façade, serves as a majestic entrance to the whole ensemble. Inside, the various pavilions are grouped around gardens that occupy an area equivalent to nine blocks of the Eixample, where both doctors and patients alike can enjoy a peaceful natural environment. The pavilions are decorated in ornate *Modernista* style using brick, colourful ceramics and natural stone. Over the years, the hospital complex has been restored several times and in 1984 it was declared a World Cultural Heritage site by UNESCO.

✉ Carrer de Sant Antoni Maria Claret 167–71
☎ 93 488 20 78 🕐 Guided tours every half hour Sat–Sun 10–2
🍴 Small coffee shop in one of the pavilions (€)
🚇 Hospital de Sant Pau 🖐 Moderate; grounds free
? Please remember that this is a hospital and not a tourist attraction

MERCAT DE LA BOQUERIA

Of more than 40 food markets in Barcelona, La Boqueria is the best and the busiest – always bustling with local shoppers, restaurateurs, gourmands and tourists. Its cavernous market hall (best entered through an imposing wrought-iron entranceway halfway up La Rambla) was built in the 1830s to house the food stalls that cluttered La Rambla and surrounding streets.

Inside is a riot of noise, perfumes and colours, with myriad stalls offering all the specialities of the Mediterranean and the Catalonian hinterland – mouth-watering displays of fruit and vegetables, a glistening array of exotic fish, endless strings of sausages and haunches of ham, and sweetly scented bunches of herbs.

Rambla 91 93 318 25 84
Mon–Sat 8am–8pm. Closed Sun & hols
Snack bars (€) Liceu
Few Free

MONESTIR DE PEDRALBES AND COLLECCIÓ THYSSEN-BORNEMISZA

The monastery of Pedralbes was founded by King Jaume II and Queen Elisenda de Montcada in 1326 to accommodate nuns of the St Clare of Assisi order. Following the king's death in 1327, Elisenda spent the last 37 years of her life here.

The spacious, three-storey cloisters are still used by the Clarista nuns. There is access to the refectory, the chapter house, the Queen's grave and St Michael's cell, with its remarkable wall murals. Baron von Thyssen-Bornemisza donated part of his priceless art collection to the monastery, with works housed in two former dormitories – mostly 13th- to 18th-century Italian and German paintings, including works by Fra Angélico, Lucas Cranach, Velázquez and Rubens .

Baixada de Monestir 9 Monastery: 93 203 92 82. Museum: 93 280 14 34 Monastery and museums: Tue–Sun 10–2. Closed Mon and hols. Church: Tue–Sun 11–1 22, 63, 64, 75 Excellent Monastery: moderate; museum: moderate Bookshop, gift shop

MONTJUÏC (➤ 26–27)

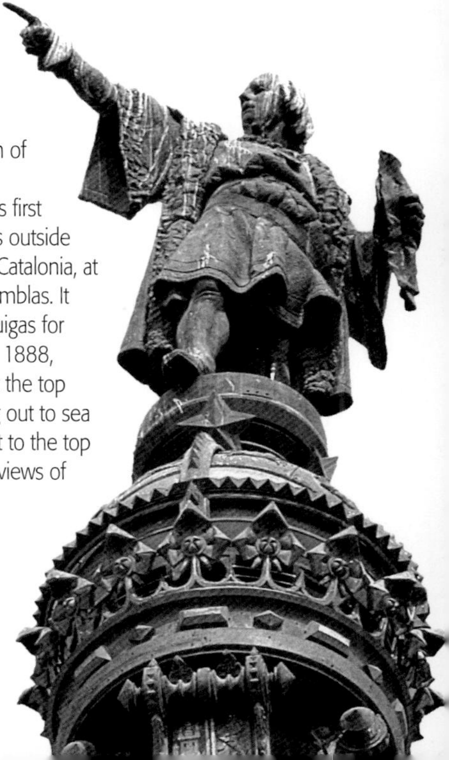

MONUMENT A COLOM

This vast monument, commemorating the return of Christopher Columbus to Barcelona in 1493 from his first trip to the Americas, stands outside the naval headquarters of Catalonia, at the seaward end of the Ramblas. It was designed by Gaietà Buigas for the Universal Exposition of 1888, with Columbus standing at the top of a 50m column, pointing out to sea – towards Italy! Take the lift to the top for breathtaking bird's-eye views of the harbourfront.

✉ Plaça Portal de la Pau
☎ 93 302 52 24
🕐 Daily Oct–May 10–6.30, Jun–Sep 9–8.30. Closed hols
🚇 Drassanes ✋ Cheap

MONTJUÏC & ANELLA OLÍMPICA
Estació Barcelona Central-Sants
Parc de l'Espanya Industrial
Parc de Joan Miró
CARRER DE TARRAGONA
GRAN VIA DE LESS CORTS CATALANES
Plaça de Toros les Arenes
RONDA DE SANT ANTONI
Palau de la Virreina
LA RAMBLA
Hospital de la Santa Creu i Sant Pau
Gran Teatre del Liceu
Palau Güell
RONDA DE SANT PAU
Drassanes & Museu Marítim
CARRER DE LA CREU COBERTA
PLAÇA D'ESPANYA
AVINGUDA DEL PARAL-LEL
HOSTAFRANCS
Fira Internacional de Mostres
Palau de Cinquantenari
POBLE SEC
GRAN VIA DE LES CORTES CATALANES
Palau de Congressos
La Font Màgica
Palau Nacional
AV MARQUÈS DE COMILAS
Fundació Joan Miró
AVINGUDA DE MIRAMAR
PASSEIG DE JOSEP CARNER
CARRETERA DE MIRAMAR
Poble Espanyol
Museu Nacional d'Art de Catalunya
Palau Albeniz
CINTURO DEL LITORAL
AVINGUDA DE L'ESTADI
Anella Olímpica
Palau d'Esports Sant Jordi
Estadi Olimpic
SANTS-MONTJUÏC
Castell de Montjuïc
CAN CLOS
Muntanya de Montjuïc
0 300 600 m
0 300 600 yards

BARCELONA ENVIRONS
Funicular al Tibidabo
PASSEIG DE LA VALL D' HEBRON
RONDA DE DALT
Vall d'Hebrón
HORTA-GUINARDO
CARRETERA D'ESPLUGUES
Museu Monestir de Pedralbes/Colleció Thyssen-Bornemisza
PEDRALBES
Museu de la Ciència
Parc de la Creueta del Coll
GRÀCIA
Parc Turó de la Peira
Palau Reial de Pedralbes
Parc Turó del Putget
RONDA DEL GENERAL MITRE
Parc Güell
Casa Museu Gaudí
LES CORTS
Area Diagonal
AVINGUDA DIAGONAL
Museu del Futbol Club Barcelona/ Camp Nou
CARRER DE CARLOS III
Parc del Guinardó
Parc de les Aigües
Jardins Poeta Eduard Marquina
Casa Vicens
CARRER DE SANTS
SANTS
Hospital de la Santa Creu i de Sant Pau
Estació Barcelona Central-Sants
Avinguda de Gaudí
GRAN VIA
Parc de l'Espanya Industrial
Hospital
L'EIXAMPLE
Sagrada Família
Hostafrancs
Parc de Joan Miró
GRAN VIA DE LES CORTS CATALANES
Manzana de la Discòrdia
AVINGUDA DE LA MERIDIANA
PASSEIG DE LA ZONA FRANCA
Parc del Clot
Poble Espanyol
PLAÇA DE CATALUNYA
Palau Nacional
POBLE SEC
EL RAVAL
Ciutat Vella
SANT PERE-RIBERA
N
Sants-Montjuïc
Muntanya de Montjuïc
Fundació Joan Miró
LA RAMBLA
Catedral
Estadi Olímpic
Museu Marítim
Casc Antic
Estació Barcelona Terme-França
Parc de la Ciutadella
POBLENOU
Castell de Montjuïc
Vila Olímpica
RONDA LITORAL
Moll de la Fusta
Palau de Mar
LA BARCELONETA
PORT OLÍMPIC
0
1
2 km
0
1 mile

MUSEU D'ART CONTEMPORANI DE BARCELONA (MACBA)

The new Barcelona Museum of Contemporary Art (MACBA), inaugurated in 1995, focuses on the art movements of the second half of the 20th century. The museum building, itself a work of art designed by the American architect Richard Meier, has been the subject of much controversy but is increasingly included as one of Barcelona's must-see landmarks. The vast white edifice with swooping ramps and glass-walled galleries almost upstages the works on display. Its location – surrounded by shabby houses in the rundown district of Raval – is intended to spearhead investment in the neighbourhood.

MACBA's extensive collection (exhibited in rotation) covers the 1940s to the 1990s, with special emphasis on Catalan and Spanish artists. It contains works by Klee, Miró and Tàpies, along with many others, including Joan Brossa, Maurizio Cattelan and Damien Hirst.

Plaça dels Àngels 1 · 93 412 08 10 · Mon–Fri 11–7.30, Sat 10–8, Sun and hols 10–3. Longer opening hours in summer. Guided tours Wed & Sat 6pm, Sun & hols 12 noon · Café (€) · Catalunya, Universitat · Excellent · Expensive

walk

Start at Plaça Portal de la Pau, with your back to the sea and Monument a Colom (➤ 77), and head up the Ramblas, beginning at La Rambla de Santa Mònica. The convent here is the only 17th-century building still standing on La Rambla.

This first section of Barcelona's famous street can be dangerous, especially at night, as it borders the Barri Xinès (China Town) district, known as a centre of drugs and crime. If you visit El Ravel after dark, take a taxi.

Continue up to Plaça del Teatre and the Rambla dels Caputxins, on the site of an ancient Capuchin convent.

This was once the heart of the old theatre district, marked by a statue of Serafi Pitarra, 'father' of contemporary theatre in Catalonia. Today, only the shabby Teatro Principal remains.

Continue north past the Gran Teatre del Liceu

ORIGINAL
EXTREME

(➤ 223) to Rambla de Sant Josep, which begins where the street widens, at Mercat de la Boqueria (➤ 74).

A meat market used to be held in the Plaça de la Boqueria. Indeed, 'boqueria' means 'butcher'. Today the square is decorated with a mosaic by Joan Miró. Flower stands line this section, commonly called the Rambla de les Flors, whereas birds and other small creatures are sold in the Rambla dels Estudis, named after a university which once stood here, although now dubbed the Rambla dels Ocells (Boulevard of the Birds).

The final Rambla – La Rambla de Canaletes, named after its famous fountain (➤ 17) – leads to Plaça de Catalunya, the square where the city's heart beats fastest (➤ 114).

Distance 1km **Time** 1 hour **Start point** Plaça Portal de la Pau Ⓜ Drassanes **End point** Plaça de Catalunya Ⓜ Catalunya **Coffee break** Café de l'Òpera (➤ 147) ✉ Rambla dels Caputxins 74 ☎ 93 302 41 80

MUSEU D'ART MODERN – MNAC

The Museum of Modern Art moved in 2004 to the National Museu of Catalan Art (➤ 24) where it completes a period spanning the 11th to 20th centuries devoted to Catalan art from the mid-19th century to around 1930.

The collection starts with works by Maria Fortuny, the earliest of the *Modernistas* and the first Catalan artist to be known widely abroad, and friends Ramon Casas and Santiago Rusinyol. The highlight of the museum is its decorative arts collection: jewellery, textiles, stained glass, ironwork, sculptures, ceramics and painted screens by Homar, Puig I Cadafalch and Gaudí, among others. The extravagance of *Modernisme* was succeeded by the less adventurous *Noucentisme* movement, which attempted to reintroduce the more harmonious values of Classical and Mediterranean art, epitomised by the works of Casanovas and Sunyer. The fascinating exhibition draws to a close with a series of striking avant-garde sculptures by Gargallo and Juli González, dating from the 1920s and 30s.

✉ Palau Nacional, Parc de Montjuïc ☎ 93 622 03 76 ⌚ Tue–Sat 10–7; Sun and hols 10–2:30. Closed Mon 🍴 Café-bar (€) Ⓜ Espanya 🚌 9, 13, 30, 50, 55 ♿ Excellent 💰 Expensive; free first Thu of month

MUSEU D'HISTÒRIA DE LA CIUTAT

The Museu d'Història de la Ciutat (City History Museum) is responsible for researching, conserving and publicising Barcelona's heritage. It is split into several sections in various locations around the Plaça del Rei (➤ 116). To start, visitors can familiarise themselves with the earliest origins of the city by wandering around the underground walkways beneath the square, which explore a vast area of excavations that have exposed the ancient Roman settlement of Barcino.

The main entrance to the museum complex is at the opposite end of the square, in Casa Padellàs, a medieval mansion which was moved here stone by stone when the Via Laietana was created in 1930. Inside, carefully chosen, thoroughly documented exhibits trace Barcelona's remarkable evolution through 2,000 years of history from a Roman trading-post to a wealthy 18th-century metropolis. Climb to the lookout point high above the galleries for memorable views.

Back in the square, a visit to the medieval buildings of the Palau Reial Major (the Great Royal Palace ➤ 116), completes the tour of the museum.

Plaça del Rei s/n 93 315 11 11 Tue–Sat 10–2, 4–8, (Jul–Sep 10–8), Sun and hols 10–2. Jaume I, Liceu Few Moderate (free 1st Sat afternoon of the month) Information service, shop and guided tours

MUSEU NACIONAL D'ART DE CATALUNYA (➤ 24–25)

MUSEU PICASSO (➤ 28–29)

MUSEU FREDERIC MARÈS

Entrance to this museum, founded by local sculptor Frederic Marès in 1946, is via a beautiful medieval courtyard, which was once part of the Royal Palace of the Kings and Queens of Catalonia and Aragon. The museum itself is divided into two main sections: the sculpture collection, featuring works from the pre-Roman period to the 20th century, and the 'Sentimental Museum', which portrays daily life from the 15th to 20th centuries through an astonishing assortment of household items. Highlights include the women's section (with collections of fans, parasols, hat pins and jewellery), the smoker's room, and the charming entertainments room, with its puppet theatres, wind-up toys and dolls.

✉ Plaça de Sant Iu 5–6 ☎ 93 310 58 00 🕒 Tue–Sat 10–7, Sun 10–3, closed hols 🍴 Summer café (€) 🚇 Jaume I ♿ Few ✋ Moderate. Free 1st Sun of month and every Wed pm ❓ Library, shop, guided visits

MUSEU TAURI DE LA MONUMENTAL

Even though bullfighting has never had a particularly passionate following in Catalonia, the Museu Tauri De La Monumental (Bullfighting Museum), located inside the Monumental Bullring, is undoubtedly one of Barcelona's more unusual museums, with its dazzling array of fancy capes and costumes, photographs, old bullfighting posters and the mounted heads of bulls.

Gran Via de les Corts Catalanes 749 93 245 58 03 Apr–Sep Mon–Sat 11–2, 4–8; Sun 11–1 Monumental Moderate

MUNDIAL
MARTINI
MARTINI
MUNDIAL

MUSEU DEL FUTBOL CLUB BARCELONA

If you can't get a ticket to see Europe's top football team in action, then at least visit the Barcelona Football Club Museum, the city's most visited museum after the revered Picasso Museum (➤ 28–29). Even those who loathe football can't help marvelling at the vast Nou Camp stadium, which seats over 98,000 spectators. The museum, under the terraces, presents a triumphant array of trophies, photographs and replays of highlights in the club's history before leading you to the shop, where everyone can buy a club shirt, pen, scarf, badge, mug. . .

✉ Nou Camp – Entrance 7 or 9, Carrer Arístides Maillol
☎ 93 496 36 00 🕐 Mon–Sat 10–6, Sun10–2, closed hols 🍴 Café (€)
🚇 Collblanc, Maria Cristina 🖐 Moderate ♿ Good ❓ Gift shop

DID YOU KNOW?

During the Franco era, FC Barcelona stood as a Catalan symbol around which people could rally, and this emotional identification remains today. It also explains why this legendary club has the world's largest soccer club membership.

MUSEU TÈXTIL I D'INDUMENTÀRIA

The Museu Tèxtil i d'Indumentària (Textile and Clothing Museum) acts as a reminder of how, thanks to its thriving textile industry, Barcelona rose to prosperity in the 1800s. It occupies a beautiful 14th-century palace, in what would then have been the aristocratic heart of Barcelona. The museum collections include textiles, tapestries, lace and clothes from medieval to modern times, with displays of textile machinery, dolls, shoes, and other fashion accessories.

✉ Carrer Montcada 12–14 ☎ 93 319 76 03 🕐 Tue–Sat 10–6, Sun and hols 10–3. Closed Mon 🍴 Café–restaurant (€) 🚇 Jaume I ♿ Good 🖐 Moderate

PALAU GÜELL

This extraordinary building, constructed in 1886–88 and declared a World Cultural Heritage site by UNESCO, was Antoni Gaudí's first major architectural project, commissioned by the Güell family.

The façade is particularly striking, with its twin arches leading into the central vestibule. Off the latter are various rooms decorated with *Modernista* fittings. A ramp leads down to the basement stables, constructed with bare-brick columns and arches. The rooftop terrace is a mixture of random spires, battlements and chimneys of differing shapes and sizes, decorated with coloured ceramic mosaics. Look closely and on one you will find a reproduction of Cobi, the 1992 Barcelona Olympics mascot. Unfortunately, the Güell family did not live here long. In 1936, the palace was confiscated by Spanish Civil War anarchists, who used it as their military headquarters and prison.

✉ Carrer Nou de la Rambla 3–5 ☎ 93 317 39 74 🕐 Mon–Sat 10–6.15. Closed Sun & hols Ⓜ Liceu ♿ None ✋ Inexpensive. Guided tours only starting every 15 minutes and lasting one hour

PALAU DE MAR

Thanks to the influence of the Olympic Games, and the opening up of the old port as a leisure area, the Palau de Mar (Palace of the Sea) – an impressive late 19th-century warehouse – has recently been converted into offices, harbourside restaurants and the spectacular Museu d'Història de Catalunya (Museum of Catalan History).

This is one of Barcelona's most sophisticated museums. Some critics have dubbed it a 'theme park', because of its lack of original exhibits, but it is nevertheless a dynamic and stimulating museum, covering the history of Catalonia in an entertaining fashion, through state-of-the-art displays, films, special effects, interactive screens and hands-on exhibits – tread an Arab waterwheel, mount a cavalier's charger, drive an early tram, take cover in a Civil War air-raid shelter…

The museum is divided into eight sections, each presenting a thorough picture of the economy, politics, technology, culture and everyday life of Catalonia over the centuries from prehistory to the restoration of democracy in 1979. The insight this innovative museum provides makes it easier for the visitor to understand the complexities of this 'nation within a nation'.

✉ Plaça Pau Vila 3, Port Vell ☎ 93 225 47 00 🕐 Tue–Sat 10–7, Wed 10–8, Sun and hols 10–2.30 🍴 Rooftop café (€) 🚇 Barceloneta ♿ Excellent 💰 Moderate (free 1st Sun of month) ❓ Gift shop, multimedia library, community programmes

PALAU DE LA MÚSICA CATALANA

In a city bursting with architectural wonders, the Palau de la Música Catalana (Palace of Catalan Music) – commissioned by the Orfeó Català (Catalan Musical Society) in 1904 and created by local architect Lluís Domènech i Montaner between 1905 and 1908 – stands out as one of Barcelona's greatest Modernist masterpieces and a symbol of the renaissance of Catalan culture.

The bare brick façade is highlighted with colourful ceramic pillars, fancy

windows and busts of Palestrina, Bach, Beethoven and Wagner. The sculptural group projecting from the corner of the building symbolises popular song. A balcony runs around the building and the main structure is supported by columns that form huge dramatic archways over the entrance.

The interior continues the ornamental theme with a profusion of decoration in the entrance hall, foyer and staircase. The pièce de résistance, however, must be the concert hall, with its exquisite roof (an inverted cupola made of stained glass), its sculptures, ceramics and paintings dedicated to musical muses (including Josep Anselm Clavé, the great 19th-century reviver of Catalan music), and its beautiful balconies and columns, designed to enhance the perspective of the auditorium.

It's no surprise that this is one of the city's main venues for classical music and it's a memorable experience to attend one of the weekly concerts; the acoustics are as fine as the surroundings.

✉ Carrer Sant Francesc de Paula 2 ☎ 93 295 72 00 🕒 Daily 10–3.30 🚇 Jaume 1, Urquinaona ♿ Few ✋ Moderate ❓ Guided tours. Early booking for concerts essential

walk

Start at the Palau Reial de Pedralbes (➤ 103). Walk eastwards along the Avinguda de la Diagonal past the Law School and turn left up Avinguda de Pedralbes.

After a short distance on the left is the former Güell Estate (No 15). Note Gaudí's extraordinary wrought-iron entrance gate, which represents a dragon.

Continue up Avinguda de Pedralbes until the T-junction. Branch left into Carretera d'Esplugues.

At No 103, the Church of Montserrat was commissioned in 1920 as a gift for the monastery of Montserrat (➤ 168) for use as a monastic foundation. The bequest was refused.

Turn right in front of the church, up Carrer Abadessa Olzet, left along Avinguda Pearson then right again up Carrer Miret i Sans as far as Carrer de Panama 21.

Here, near the corner (No 21), a charming medieval farmhouse underlines the former rural character of Pedralbes. By contrast, No 13, a *Modernista* mansion with a gleaming polychromatic tiled roof, reflects the wealth of this district.

The road turns into Carrer de Montevideo and passes behind the monastery of Pedralbes (➤ 76), hidden behind bougainvillaea-smothered walls. A flight of steps leads down Baixada del Monestir, past a small, leafy square, to the main entrance.

Distance 3km **Time** 1 hour (excluding visits) **Start point** Palau Reial de Pedralbes Palau Reial **End point** Monestir de Pedralbes 22, 63, 64, 75, 78

PALAU REIAL DE PEDRALBES

The Palau Reial de Pedralbes (Royal Palace of Pedralbes) accommodated the Spanish royal family during the International Exhibition of 1929 and, after 1939, became Franco's residence on visits to the city. The gardens were landscaped by Nicolau Rubió i Turdurí, who integrated the existing trees into his design, and there is a fountain by Gaudí.

Today the state rooms house two museums. The Museu de Ceràmica traces the development of Spanish ceramics from the 12th century onwards, and includes the 18th-century Catalan panels *La Cursa de Braus* (the Bullfight) and *La Xocolotada* (the Chocolate Party), together with works by Picasso and Miró. The Museu de les Arts Decoratives has an impressive collection of decorative arts that spans the early Middle Ages to the present day.

✉ Avinguda de la Diagonal 686 ☎ Museu de les Arts Decoratives: 93 280 50 24. Museu de Ceràmica: 93 280 16 21 🕔 Tue–Sun 10–6 (park 10–sunset) Ⓜ Palau Reial 🚌 7, 33, 67, 68, 74, 75 ♿ Museu d'Arts Decoratives: good; Museu de Ceràmica: few ✋ Museums: moderate (free 1st Sun of month); park: free ? Shop, library, guided visits, educational services

PARC DE LA CIUTADELLA

This delightful walled park is a haven of shade and tranquillity just a stone's throw from the old city and waterfront. What's more, hidden among the trees, lawns, promenades and a boating lake, you'll find the Parc Zoològic (► 216) and a host of other attractions. This is a great place to relax and people-watch on a pleasant Sunday afternoon.

In 1888 the park was the site of the Universal Exposition and still contains some impressive relics of that great fair, including a striking *Modernista* café which now houses the **Museu de Zoologia**, with highlights that include a fascinating Whale Room and a Sound Library of recordings of animal sounds.

Near by, the neoclassical **Museu de Geologia**, with its rare and valuable minerals, fossils and rocks, opened in 1878 as Barcelona's first public museum. The impressive Hivernacle greenhouse, originally built for the display of exotic plants, is today a popular café (► 149), but the main showpiece of the park is the Font Monumental – a huge, neoclassical-style fountain, smothered in allegorical sculptures, which Gaudí contributed to as a student.

Outside the park on Passeig Lluís Companys, the monumental Arc de Triomf was constructed by Josep Vilaseca i Casanovas as the grand entrance to the Universal Exhibition.

Main entrance: Passeig Lluís Companys Ciutadella, Arc de Triomf, Barceloneta, Jaume I Good Free

Museu de Zoologia

Passeig de Picasso 93 319 69 12 Tue–Sun 10–2 (Thu until 6.30) Moderate

Museu de Geologia

Parc de la Ciutadella 93 319 68 95 Tue–Sun 10–2 (Thu until 6.30) Moderate

PARC DE L'ESPANYA INDUSTRIAL

With works by many Catalan artists, this is Barcelona's most controversial park – a *nou urbanisme* project, built between 1982 and 1985 on the site of an old textile factory. It is built on two levels, the lower part comprising a large lake and grassy area, with steep white steps up to the much-scorned upper esplanade, where there are ten lighthouses, a series of water spouts and an immense metal play-sculpture entitled the *Dragon of St George*.

Carrer de Muntadas Sants-Estació
Free

PARC GÜELL (➤ 21–23)

PARC DEL CLOT

This park in the eastern suburbs has been built on the site of a disused railway yard and combines the walls and arches of the former rail buildings with a low-lying playing-field (the name 'Clot' in Catalan means 'hole') and a shady *plaça*, linked to a high grassy area of artificial hills and enigmatic sculptures by a lengthy overhead walkway.

✉ Carrer Escultors Claperós 🕓 Nov–Feb 10–6; Mar and Oct 10–7; Apr and Sep 10–8; May–Aug 10–9 🚇 Clot, Glories ✋ Free

PARC DE LA CREUETA DEL COLL

This new park was built in a disused quarry by Olympic architects Martorell and Mackay in 1987. Surrounded by dramatic cliff-faces, scattered with modern sculptures and embracing wooded pathways and a small sand-fringed boating lake, it serves the densely inhabited suburb of Vallcarca and is always packed in summer.

✉ Passeig Mare de Déu del Coll 🕓 10–sunset 🚌 25, 28, 87 ✋ Free

PARC DE JOAN MIRÓ

Somewhat rundown these days, but enduringly popular, this park occupies an entire city block on what was formerly the site of a massive abattoir, hence its nickname Parc de l'Escorxador (slaughterhouse). It was created in the 1980s, and is always full of people reading, jogging, dog-walking or playing *petanca* (boules) amid the attractive pergolas and orderly rows of shady palm trees. The park's most famous feature, however, is a startling 22m-high sculpture by Joan Miró, covered in multicoloured ceramic fragments, named *Dona i Ocell* (Woman and Bird).

Carrer de Tarragona Snack bar Tarragona, Espanya 9, 13, 27, 30, 38, 50, 53, 56, 57, 65, 91, 109, 157 Free

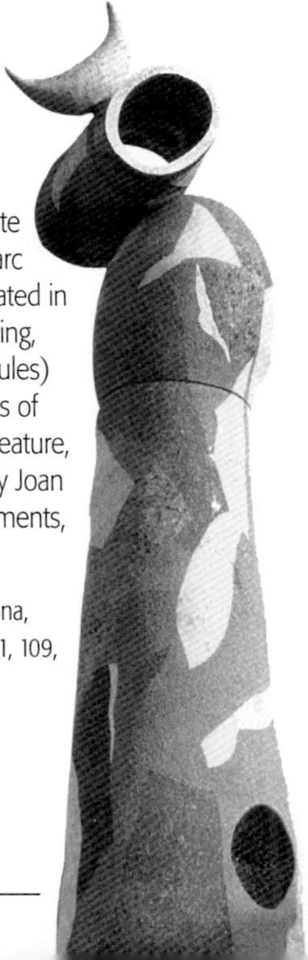

PARC DEL LABERINT

These romantic, Italian-style gardens, on the wooded outer rim of Barcelona near the Vall d'Hebrón, present a pleasing contrast to the stark modern *espais urbans* (urban spaces) of

the city centre. They originally surrounded a grand 18th-century mansion, which has long since been demolished, but the park has maintained its formal flowerbeds, canals and fountains, its ornamental statuary and its centrepiece – the 'Labyrinth' – a beautiful topiary maze with a statue of Eros at its centre that has given the park its name.

Passeig dels Castanyers or Carrer Germans Desvalls, Vall d'Hebron Daily 10 until dark, ticket office closes one hour before closing time Mundet
10, 27, 60, 73, 76, 85 Inexpensive; free Wed and Sun

PAVELLÓ MIES VAN DER ROHE

Bauhaus architect Ludwig Mies van der Rohe created this masterpiece of modern rationalist design for the 1929 Exhibition, a construction of astonishing simplicity and finesse in marble, onyx, glass and chrome, widely acknowledged as one of the classic buildings of the 20th century. It was dismantled at the end of the fair and subsequently meticulously reconstructed and reopened (in its original location) in 1986, on the centenary of Mies van der Rohe's birth.

Inside, take time to enjoy the quality of the colours, textures and materials, as well as a striking bronze sculpture entitled *Der Morgen* (The Morning) and the famous 'Barcelona' chair, a design of timeless elegance created especially for the Expo, which has since been copied worldwide.

✉ Avinguda del Marquès de Comillas s/n ☎ 93 423 40 16
🕘 Daily 10–8 🚇 Espanya 🚌 27, 50, 91, 157 ♿ Good
🎫 Inexpensive

PLAÇA DE CATALUNYA

The Plaça de Catalunya is the heart of Barcelona and the hub of the city's transport system. It was first landscaped at the end of the 19th century and soon became of major importance as the pivotal point between the old and new city, with the Barri Gòtic (➤ 58–61) to the east, the planned new Eixample district (➤ 64–64) to the north and west, and, to the southeast, La Rambla (➤ 16–17) running down to the port.

In 1927 the square was further developed, with the construction of hotels and restaurants. Its main landmarks are the head office of Banco Espanol de Crédito, former headquarters of the unified Socialist Party of Catalonia during the Civil War; the monstrous El Corte Inglés department store; and a medley of fountains and statues. Today, its benches, trees and splashing fountains make it a popular place to meet friends and have a coffee or simply to sit and soak up the sun.

Several (€–€€) Catalunya

HOTEL BARCELONA

PLAÇA DEL REI

The charming King's Square was once a bustling medieval marketplace. Today, it forms a frequent backdrop to summer open-air concerts and theatrical events, especially during the Grec festival (➤ 229), and is the location not only of the City History Museum (➤ 86–87) but also of the **Palau Reial Major** (Great Royal Palace), former residence of the Counts of Barcelona.

It was on the steps leading up to the Palau Reial Major that King Ferdinand and Queen Isabella are said to have received Columbus on his return from his first voyage to America in 1493. Inside, the Spanish Inquisition once sat in the Saló del Tinell, exploiting the local myth that should any prisoner lie, the stones on the ceiling would move. Today, the hall functions as an exhibition area.

On the north side of the square is the chapel of Santa Agata (also part of the royal palace), which contains a precious 15th-century altarpiece by Jaume Huguet. On the opposite side of the square, the Palau de Lloctinent (Palace of the Deputy) was built in 1549 for the Catalan representative of the king in Madrid. The strenuous climb to the top of its five-storey

lookout tower (the Mirador del Rei Martí) is well rewarded by sweeping views of the old town.

Jaume I

Palau Reial Major

93 315 11 11 Palace: Tue–Sat 10–2, 4–8, Sun and hols 10–3; tower: temporarily closed for restoration

Moderate Part of the Museu d'Historia de la Ciutat (➤ 86–87)

pardo
pardo
pardo

PLAÇA REIAL

This sunny porticoed square, just off the Ramblas, with its tall palm trees, decorative fountain and buskers was constructed in 1848. Some of the façades are decorated with terracotta reliefs of navigators and the discoverers of America, and the two tree-like central lamp posts mark Gaudí's first commission in Barcelona.

Keep a close watch on your belongings here – the square has a reputation for shady characters and pickpockets, hence the discreet but constant police presence. On Sunday mornings a coin and stamp market is held here.

Plenty (€–€€) Liceu or Drassanes

PLAÇA SANT JAUME

Once the hub of Roman Barcelona, this impressive square today represents the city's political heart, and is dominated by two buildings; the neoclassical and Gothic Casa de la Ciutat (Town Hall) and, directly opposite, the Renaissance Palau de la Generalitat de Catalunya (Government of Catalonia).

In 1249 Jaume I granted Barcelona the right to elect councillors, giving rise to the creation of the Consell de Cent (Council of One Hundred). The famous Saló de Cent (Chamber of One Hundred) and the black marble Saló de las Cronicas (Chamber of the Chronicles) are among the architectural highlights of the Town Hall.

Cafés (€) Jaume I

POBLE ESPANYOL (➤ 36–37)

walk

Start on Moll de les Drassanes near the Columbus Monument (➤ 77), then head along Passeig del Moll de la Fusta by the water's edge.

Raised on stilts above the yacht basin, the Passeig de Colom was Barcelona's most stylish promenade when it opened in 1987, with designer restaurants and bars and a giant rooftop lobster sculpture. These days many of the trendier restaurants have closed down and most of the action has moved to Port Vell (➤ 124) and the Port Olímpic (➤ 45), but it still makes an interesting scene.

Continue walking northeast until Plaça d'Antoni López.

This busy square is dominated by the main post office (Correos y Telegrafos) and a notable mosaic sculpture by Roy Lichtenstein.

Leave the square via the arcaded walkway of Passeig d'Isabel II, past the Stock Exchange and the famous '7 Doors' (Set Portes) restaurant (➤ 140), and turn right at Pla de Palau. Cross the main road into La Barceloneta

(► 45) and continue along the waterfront, past the Palau de Mar (► 96) with its fish restaurants, until you reach Passeig de Joan de Borbó.

Note the wide variety of architectural styles here, especially No 43, which is one of the best examples of 1950s architecture in Barcelona. To your right, the clock tower by the harbour was originally a lighthouse, and the Torre de Sant Sebastià on Moll Nou once carried cable-cars, via the Jaume I Tower, to Montjuïc.

On reaching the seafront, turn left on to Passeig Marítim, which runs parallel to the beach all the way to the Port Olímpic, heralded by a massive, gleaming fish sculpture by Frank Gehry (► 45).

Distance 3 km **Time** 2–3 hours (excluding visits)
Start point Monument a Colom Ⓜ Drassanes
End point Port Olímpic Ⓜ Ciutadella
Lunch break Emperador (€€€) (► 95)
✉ Palau de Mar, Plaça Pau Vila ☎ 93 221 02 20

PORT VELL

Although Barcelona was founded on sea-going tradition, for many years its seafront was in decay, until a major redevelopment prior to the 1992 Olympics reintegrated the Port Vell (Old Port) into the city by transforming it into a lively new entertainment venue. The Rambla de Mar, a series of undulating wooden walkways and bridges, acts as an extension of La Rambla, connecting the city to Port Vell's many new attractions.

Maremagnum, Port Vell's biggest crowd puller, is a covered shopping and entertainment centre with smart boutiques, expensive restaurants, trendy bars, discos and fast-food joints. Adjacent to the conventional cinema complex, IMAX, the 'cinema of the future', shows spectacular films in three dimensions, with state-of-the-art wrap-around screens and sound. Near by, the Aquarium (➤ 214), one of the biggest and best in Europe, always proves popular with children.

Take a *golondrina* (pleasure boat) for a different perspective of the new harbour developments. The luxurious leisure marina, with more than 400 berths, in the previously derelict dockyard area is rapidly becoming one of the Mediterranean's most exclusive anchorages. Although the big ferries to the Balearics still depart from here, most commercial activity now takes place in the modern port farther down the coast.

Cafés, bars and restaurants (€–€€€) Drassanes, Barceloneta
Free

LA RAMBLA (➤ 16–17)

SAGRADA FAMÍLIA (➤ 30–31)

SANTA MARIA DEL MAR (➤ 34–35)

TIBIDABO AND SERRA DE COLLSEROLA

The 550m-high Mont Tibidabo forms the northwestern boundary of Barcelona and boasts panoramic views over the entire city, and, on exceptionally clear days, Mallorca.

At its summit, and topped by a huge statue of Christ, stands the modern Church of the Sacred Heart (Sagrat Cor), whose style is best described as 'neo-Gothic fantasy'. Near by, the 'Magic Mountain' **Amusement Park** (➤ 217) cleverly balances traditional rides with high-tech attractions on several levels of the mountaintop, and is always a fun day out for the family. Tibidabo is just one of the mountains of the Collserola range, a 6,550ha nature reserve with woodlands full of wildlife. It is best reached by FGC train to Baixador de Vallvidrera. From here, it is a 10-minute walk uphill to the information centre, where details of itineraries for walkers and cyclists are available.

Cafés, snack bars (€–€€) FGC Avinguda Tibidabo then Tramvia Blau to Plaça Doctor Andreu followed by the Tibidabo Funicular
Free.

Amusement Park www.tibidabo.es

Where to eat & drink... Barcelona

RESTAURANTS

OLD CITY

ABAC (€€€)

The elegance, spaciousness and minimalism of Abac's stylish cream-and-orange dining room provides a perfect backdrop for the fine Spanish haute cuisine of local chef Xavier Pellicier.

✉ Carrer Rec 79–89 ☎ 93 319 66 00 🕐 Closed Sun, Aug and Mon mid-Sep 🚇 Barceloneta

AGUT D'AVIGNON (€€€)

Hidden up an alleyway off Calle d'Avinyó at the heart of the Barri Gòtic, with classic Catalan cuisine that attracts politicians, artists, and even the King of Spain.

✉ Carrer Trinitat 3 ☎ 93 302 60 34 🚇 Jaume I

AMAYA (€€€)

Popular Basque restaurant, featuring *angulas* (baby eels) and *besugo* (sea bream). Wash them down with one of the many regional wines.

La Rambla 20–24 93 302 10 37 Liceu

BIO-CENTER (€)

The best-known of Barcelona's very few vegetarian restaurants, the Bio-Center serves a range of delicious soups, casseroles and salads.

Carrer Pintor Fortuny 25 93 301 45 83 Mon–Sat 1–5 Catalunya

BRASSERIE FLO (€€)

Famous French-founded brasserie. House specialities include *foie gras* and Alsatian-style ham with *choucroute* (sauerkraut).

Carrer Jonqueres 10 93 319 31 02 Urquinaona

CAFÉ DE L'ACADEMIA (€€)

One of Barcelona's best-value restaurants, with generous helpings of delicious Mediterranean cuisine in the heart of the old city.

Carrer Lledó 1 93 315 00 26 Closed weekends and 2 weeks Aug Jaume I

CAN CULLERETES (€€)

One of the oldest restaurants in the city (1786), traditionally decorated with wrought-iron chandeliers and signed photographs of visiting celebrities. Among the highlights of the Catalan cuisine on the menu is *perdiz* (partridge).

Carrer Quintana 5 93 317 30 22 Lunch: Tue–Sun 1.30–4; dinner: Tue–Sat 9–11pm. Closed 3 weeks Jul Liceu

CA L'ISIDRE (€€€)

Sophisticated bistro offering exceptional Catalan cuisine and an extensive wine list.

Carrer Les Flors 120 93 441 11 39 Closed Sun and hols Paral.lel (best by taxi)

LOS CARACOLES (€€)

Popular with both tourists and locals, and particularly famous for its robust, country-style cuisine, especially the spit-roasted chicken, and its namesake, snails.

Carrer Escudellers 14 93 302 31 85 Drassanes, Liceu

CASA LEOPOLDO (€€€)

Family-run seafood restaurant, in seedy location in the Barri Xinés: arrive by taxi! Its tapas bar is also hugely popular.

✉ Carrer Sant Rafael 24 ☎ 93 441 30 14 🕒 Tue–Sat 1.30–4, 9–11; Sun 1.30–4 🚇 Liceu

LA CUINETA (€€)

Well-established restaurant in the Barri Gòtic, serving authentic dishes from northeastern Spain. Good-value fixed-price menu.

✉ Carrer Pietat 12 ☎ 93 315 01 11 🚇 Jaume 1

EGIPTE (€€)

This small restaurant on La Rambla serves good-value Catalan cuisine such as cod in a cream sauce or stuffed aubergine.

✉ La Rambla 79 ☎ 93 317 95 45 🚇 Liceu

L'EUCALIPTUS (€)

A traditional tiled brasserie, offering a simple menu of *torradas* (toasted open sandwiches) and *escalivada* (traditional pepper and aubergine dish) just off La Rambla.

✉ Carrer Bonsuccés 4 ☎ 93 302 18 24 🕒 Closed Sun eves and Mon 🚇 Catalunya

LA FONDA (€–€€)

One of Ciutat Vella's most popular restaurants, with good, yet affordable Catalan food in stylish surroundings.

✉ Carrer Escudellers 10 ☎ 93 301 75 15 Ⓜ Liceu

LA GARDUNYA (€)

Impressive seafood platters and an excellent-value *menú del día* at this celebrated restaurant in the Boqueria market.

✉ Carrer Jerusalem 18 ☎ 93 302 43 23 ⏲ Closed Sun Ⓜ Liceu

EL GRAN CAFÉ (€€)

Classic restaurant, serving French and Catalan cuisine in grand turn-of-the-19th-century surroundings.

✉ Carrer d'Avinyó 9 ☎ 93 318 79 86 ⏲ Closed Sun Ⓜ Liceu

HOFMANN (€€€)

Interpretations of regional dishes by Mey Hofmann, one of Spain's most talented chefs, who also runs a world-renowned cookery school on the premises.

✉ Carrer Argenteria 74–78 ☎ 93 319 58 89 ⏲ Closed Sat, Sun and Aug Ⓜ Jaume I ? Phone for details of special two-day cookery courses

L'OU COM BALLA (€€)

Hidden down a back street of La Ribera near Santa Maria del Mar, the friendly staff at this cosy restaurant serve culinary delights, including a variety of regional dishes.

Carrer Banys Vells 20
93 310 53 78 Jaume I

EL PARAGUAYO (€€)

Specialities from Paraguay and Argentina, including barbecued meat served on wooden boards, and salads and pastas.

Carrer Parc 1 93 302 14 41
Closed Mon Drassanes

LA PERLA NERA (€€)

Authentic flavours, perfect pastas and an attractive dining room, brimming with fresh flowers are the trademark of this well-respected Italian restaurant.

Via Laietana 32–4 93 310 56 46 Jaume I

EL PINTOR (€€)

Serving traditional Catalan cuisine and fine regional wines, the interior is cosy with crisp white linen and candlelight.

✉ Carrer St Honorat 7 ☎ 93 301 40 65 Ⓜ Jaume I

PITARRA (€)

An old-fashioned Spanish restaurant in the Barri Gòtic. They serve a particularly good Valencian paella.

✉ Carrer d'Avinyó 56 ☎ 93 301 16 47 🕐 Closed Sun and Aug Ⓜ Liceu

ELS QUATRE GATS (€€)

Famous artists and intellectuals gathered in this *Modernista* café in the early 1900s. The menu was designed by Picasso.

✉ Carrer Montsió 3 bis ☎ 93 302 41 40 Ⓜ Catalunya

LES QUINZE NITS (€€)

Under the same management as La Fonda (► 132), this wood-panelled restaurant with an attractive terrace serves an excellent Catalan-style *civet de conill* (rabbit stew) and an impressive *parillada de peix* (seafood mixed grill).

✉ Plaça Reial 6 ☎ 93 317 30 75 Ⓜ Liceu

QUO VADIS (€€€)

One of Barcelona's finest restaurants, near the Boqueria market, serving time-tested recipes from all over Spain.

✉ Carrer Carme 7 ☎ 93 302 40 72 🕐 Closed Sun and Aug
🚇 Liceu

LA RIOJA (€–€€)

This bright restaurant offers a good-value *menú del día*.

✉ Carrer Duran i Bas 5 ☎ 93 301 22 98
🕐 Closed Sat eve, Sun and Aug 🚇 Catalunya

SUSHI-YA (€€)

Small Japanese restaurant, serving the usual sushi, sashimi, tempura and *miso* soup.

✉ Carrer Quintana 4 ☎ 93 412 72 49
🚇 Liceu

TAXIDERMISTA (€€)

Buzzy designer restaurant in an old taxidermist's studio, offering modern Mediterranean dishes such as lamb couscous or duck breast with truffle vinaigrette.

Plaça Reial 8 93 412 45 36 Closed Mon and 3 weeks Aug Liceu

VENUS (€–€€)

This bright, cheerful neighbourhood bar prides itself on its authentic cuisine from all around the Mediterranean basin.

Carrer Avinyó 25 93 301 15 85 Jaume 1

SEAFRONT

AGUA (€€)

Located right on the Barceloneta beach, near the Port Olímpic. The menu offers excellent traditional Barceloneta fare, with the emphasis on rice-based dishes.

Passeig Marítim de la Barceloneta 30 93 225 12 72 Ciutadella

BESTIAL (€€)

Great Italian bistro with wood decking, palm trees and parasol topped tables, all with views of Frank Gehry's golden fish.

Carrer Ramon Trias Fargas 2–4 93 224 04 07 Ciutadella-Vila Olímpica

CAL PINXO (€€€)

Fashionable seafood restaurant facing Barceloneta beach, where paella and fish dishes can be enjoyed on a terrace.

✉ Carrer Baluard 124 ☎ 93 221 50 28 Ⓜ Barceloneta

EL CANGREJO LOCO (€€)

Popular fish restaurant at the far end of the Port Olímpic but worth the walk for its extensive *pica-pica* starters and delicious main dishes – try the *fideua*, cod fried in honey.

✉ Moll de Gregal 29–30, Port Olímpic ☎ 93 221 05 33 Ⓜ Ciutadella

CAN MAJÓ (€€€)

The city's top seafood restaurant, in La Barceloneta. The *suquet de peix* (mixed fish casserole), *arrozes* (black rice) with *bacalao* (salt cod) are truly delicious.

✉ Carrer Almirall Aixada 23 ☎ 93 221 54 55 🕐 Closed Sun eve and Mon Ⓜ Barceloneta

EMPERADOR (€€€)

One of the best of the new harbourside restaurants in the fashionable Palau de Mar.

✉ Palau de Mar, Plaça Pau Vila 1 ☎ 93 221 02 20 Ⓜ Barceloneta

JULIUS (€€€)

Up-market, Scandinavian styled bar serving first class fish and seafood tapas, and delicious rice dishes.

✉ Passeig Joan de Borbó 66
☎ 93 224 70 35
Ⓜ Barceloneta

EL PASSADÍS D'EL PEP (€€€)

There's no menu as such here, just some of the best fish in town. Choose from bream, bass, oysters, shellfish or the catch of the day.

✉ Pla del Palau 2 ☎ 93 310 10 21 🕓 Closed Sun, hols and 3 weeks Aug Ⓜ Barceloneta

SAN FERMÍN (€€)

Rustic Basque restaurant by Port Olímpic. Cider is poured from the barrel and T-bone steaks are cooked on an outdoor grill.

✉ Moll de Gregal 22 ☎ 93 221 05 43 Ⓜ Ciutadella

SET PORTES (€€€)

One of Barcelona's most historic restaurants, with waiters in long white aprons, serving excellent Catalan cuisine.

✉ Passeig de Isabel II, 14 ☎ 93 319 30 33 Ⓜ Barceloneta

EIXAMPLE & GRÀCIA

ASADOR DE BURGES (€€€)

A traditional Castilian roast house where lamb and suckling pig are cooked in a brick oven until they are tender to the touch.

✉ Carrer Bruc 118 ☎ 93 207 31 60 🕐 Closed Sun; Mon and Tue evening Ⓜ Verdaguer

BELTXENEA (€€€)

Barcelona's premier Basque restaurant is set in an elegant 19th-century *Modernista* building.

✉ Carrer Mallorca 275 ☎ 93 215 30 24 🕐 Closed Sat lunch, all day Sun, Aug and public hols Ⓜ Diagonal, Passeig de Gràcia

BOTAFUMEIRO (€€€)

This Galician seafood restaurant serves fish (flown in daily from Galicia) with regional wines and Catalan *cavas*. The *mariscos Botafumeira* (seafood platter) is a sight to behold.

✉ Carrer de Gran de Gràcia 81 ☎ 93 218 42 30 Ⓜ Fontana

EL CABALLITO BLANCO (€)

The 'Little White Horse' is a cheerful, good-value, traditional restaurant, always packed with locals.

✉ Carrer Mallorca 196 ☎ 93 453 10 33 🕐 Closed Sun eve, Mon and Aug Ⓜ Hospital Clinic

CASI CASI (€)

An Andalusian restaurant in Gracia. Try the excellent gazpacho or *ajoblanco* (cold garlic soup) to start, followed by the daily catch a *la Andaluza*.

✉ Carrer Laforja 8 ☎ 93 415 81 94 Ⓜ Gràcia

CASA CALVET (€€€)

Gaudí's first apartment building in Barcelona is now a formal restaurant offering sophisticated French and Catalan cuisine.

✉ Carrer Casp 48 ☎ 93 412 40 12 🕐 Closed Sun Ⓜ Urquinaona

LA DAMA (€€€)

The French cuisine of this Michelin star-rated restaurant rivals that of the top restaurants of Paris.

✉ Avinguda Diagonal 423 ☎ 93 202 06 86 🚇 Provença

FRESCCO (€)

Eat-as-much-as-you-want from the self-service salads, pasta, pizza, ice cream, bread and beverages. Take-away service also available.

✉ Carrer València 263 ☎ 93 488 10 49 🚇 Passeig de Gràcia

EL GLOP (€)

Crowded restaurant serving chargrilled meat at reasonable prices, washed down with Catalan wines.

✉ Carrer Sant Lluís 24 (also at Carrer Casp 21 and Rambla Catalunya 65) ☎ 93 213 70 58 🕒 Closed Mon 🚇 Joanic

JEAN LUC FIGUERAS (€€€)

Exquisite culinary delights served in striking surroundings and enhanced by original art deco silverware.

✉ Carrer Santa Teresa 10 ☎ 93 415 28 77 🕒 Closed Sun, 3 weeks Aug 🚇 Diagonal

MADRID-BARCELONA (€€)

Charming café-restaurant where dishes are served *a la brasa* – cooked on a coal-fired range.

✉ Carrer d'Aragó 282 ☎ 93 215 70 27 ⊙ Closed Sun Ⓜ Passeig de Gràcia

MANDALAY-CAFÉ (€€)

Fun and funky, this restaurant fuses Thai, Vietnamese and Indonesian cuisine with Mediterranean ingredients and entertains with trapeze artists on Fridays and Saturdays.

✉ Carrer Provenca 330 ☎ 93 458 60 17 Ⓜ Verdaguer, Diagonal

EL RACÓ D'EN FREIXA (€€€)

Highly original cooking makes this one of the city's most popular Sunday-lunch haunts. Save room for the puddings which come in threes – bananas, fried, baked and caramelised, or a trio of iced, warm and hot chocolate delights.

✉ Carrer Sant Elies 22 ☎ 93 209 75 59 ⊙ Closed Sun, Mon & Aug Ⓜ Plaça Molina/Sant Gervasi

SUBURBS

ALKIMIA (€€€)

Barcelona's most exciting new comer with chef Jordi Vila at the helm, serving wonderfully innovative dishes.

✉ Carrer Industria 79 ☎ 93 207 61 15 Ⓜ Verdaguer, Hospital Sant Pau, Sagrada Familia

LA BALSA (€€€)

International cuisine served at the top of this circular tower, originally built as a water cistern.

✉ Carrer Infanta Isabel 4, Sant Gervasi ☎ 93 211 50 48 Ⓒ Closed Mon lunch, Aug lunch & Sun Ⓜ Tibidabo

LA BODEGUITA DEL POBLE (€€)

One of several theme restaurants in the Poble Espanyol, this one offers Cuban market cooking such as pork, beans and rice.

✉ Poble Espanyol ☎ 93 426 38 45 🚌 13, 50, 61

CAN TRAVINOU (€€€)

Set in a beautiful 18th-century *masìa* (farmhouse) and garden, on a hill above Horta. The wine list extends to 500 wines and *cavas*.

✉ Carrer Jorge Manrique s/n ☎ 93 428 03 01 🕓 Closed Sun eve
🚇 Montbau

GAIG (€€€)

Famous family-run restaurant, founded in 1869 as a café for cart drivers, now one of Barcelona's smartest eateries.

✉ Passeig Maragall 402 ☎ 93 429 10 17 🕓 Closed Sun eve, Mon & 3 weeks Aug 🚇 Vilapicina

NEICHEL (€€€)

This stylish restaurant boasts the talents of Alsace-born chef Jean-Louis Neichel, who has been described as 'the most brilliant ambassador French cuisine has ever had within Spain'.

✉ Carrer Beltrán í Rózpide 16 bis ☎ 93 203 84 08 🕓 Closed Sun, Mon, Aug and hols 🚇 Palau Reial

LA PARRA (€–€€)

Country cooking in an old coaching inn with hearty portions of lamb, rabbit, steak and spare ribs cooked on a giant wood-fired grill, and served with lashings of homemade *allioli*.

✉ Carrer Joanot Martorell 3, Hostafranca ☎ 93 332 51 34 🕓 Closed Aug, Mon, Tue–Fri lunch and Sun eve 🚇 Hostafranca

LA VENTA (€€€)

The conservatory and terrace, and the light, imaginative menu, make for perfect spring lunches and relaxing summer evenings.

✉ Plaça Dr Andreu, Sant Gervasi ☎ 93 212 64 55 🕐 Closed Sun 🚇 Avinguda Tibidabo then Tramvia Blau

CAFÉS AND TAPAS BARS

OLD CITY

AMBOS MUNDOS

Pleasant *cerveceria* (beer bar) in Plaça Reial serving wholesome tapas in terracotta dishes.

✉ Plaça Reial 9–10 ☎ 93 317 01 66 🕐 Closed Tue eve 🚇 Liceu

BAR DEL PI

Simple but popular, despite its small tapas selection, in one of Barcelona's most atmospheric squares.

✉ Plaça Sant Josep Oriol 1 ☎ 93 302 21 23 🕐 Closed Tue, 2 weeks Jan and 2 weeks Aug 🚇 Liceu

EL BOSC DE LES FADES

An extraordinary café-cum-magic fairy world, decorated with fountains, toadstools and fairytale princesses.

✉ Passatge de la Banca, La Rambla 4–6 ☎ 93 317 26 49 Ⓜ Drassanes

CAFÈ DE L'ÒPERA

This original 19th-century café is one of Barcelona's favourites, and the best terrace-café along the Ramblas.

✉ La Rambla 74 ☎ 93 302 41 80 Ⓜ Liceu

CAFÉ ZURICH

Popular bar and meeting place at the top of La Rambla. Great for people-watching and soaking up the atmosphere.

✉ Plaça Catalunya 1 ☎ 93 317 91 53 Ⓜ Catalunya

CELTA

A Galician bar near the port, known for its fried *rabas* (squid) and its *patatas bravas*, (potatoes in a spicy mayonnaise), serving Galician white wine in traditional white ceramic cups.

Carrer Mercè 16 · 93 315 00 06 · Closed Sun · Drassanes, Barceloneta

DULCINEA

The most famous chocolate shop in town. Try *melindros* (sugar-topped sponge fingers) dipped in very thick hot chocolate.

Carrer Petritxol 2 · 93 302 68 24 · Liceu

FORN DE BETLEM

A bright orange, trendy café and cake shop near the Museum of Contemporary Art, one of very few places around the museum where you can stop for a coffee or a snack.

Carrer Joaquín Costa 34 · Universitat

HARD ROCK CAFÉ

The latest addition to the world-famous chain.

Plaça de Catalunya 21 · 93 270 23 05 · Catalunya

HIVERNACLE

Elegant café inside the Parc de la Ciutadella's beautiful 19th-century greenhouse. Occasional live jazz or classical music.

✉ Parc de la Ciutadella ☎ 93 295 40 17 🕐 Closed Sun eve
🚇 Arc de Triomf

IRATI

One of the city's best-loved bars for sumptuous *pintxos* (Basque tapas) washed down with *txacoli* (Basque country semi-sparkling wine) and the locally brewed cider.

✉ Carrer Cardenal Casañas 17 ☎ 93 302 30 84 🚇 Liceu

MESÓN DEL CAFÉ

Join locals at the bar for a coffee or hot chocolate while exploring the Barri Gòtic.

✉ Carrer de la Llibreteria 16 ☎ 93 315 07 54
🕐 Closed Sun 🚇 Jaume I

LA PLATA

One of several *tascas* (traditional bars) on this narrow medieval street, specialising in whitebait, anchovies, and tomato and onion salads.

✉ Carrer Mercè 28 ☎ 93 315 10 09 ⏲ Closed Sun Ⓜ Barceloneta

SAGARDI

Spacious bar, popular with the young pre-dinner crowd, or for those wishing to make a meal out of their large, tasty tapas.

✉ Carrer Argenteria 62 ☎ 93 319 99 93 ⏲ Closed Sat Ⓜ Jaume I

TÈXTIL CAFÈ

Delicious quiches and salads, in the courtyard of the medieval palace which houses the Museu Tèxtil.

✉ Carrer Montcada 12 ☎ 93 268 25 98 ⏲ Closed Mon Ⓜ Jaume I

? No need to pay museum entrance

LA VINYA DEL SENYOR

A modern, stand-up wine bar beside Santa Maria del Mar.
✉ Plaça Santa Maria 5 ☎ 93 310 33 79 🕒 Closed Mon 🚇 Jaume I

SEAFRONT

CAN RAMONET

This is a stand-up tapas bar in one of La Barceloneta's top fish restaurants. It is worth trying their mussels, 'from the beach'.
✉ Carrer Maquinista 17 ☎ 93 319 30 64 🚇 Barceloneta

FORN DE BETLEM

This tucked away bakery serves a range of rustic loaves from Finnish multi-grains to German rye, as well as a great range of sandwiches and snacks to takeaway. Perfect for picnics.
✉ Carrer Xuclà 23 ☎ 93 302 27 82 🕒 Mon-Sat 7am-9pm
🚇 Catalunya

EL REY DE LA GAMBA

The 'King of Prawns' serves seafood and cured hams. Busy at weekends.
✉ Passeig Joan de Borbó 53 (also Moll Mistral, Port Olímpic)
☎ 93 221 73 06 🚇 Barceloneta

EIXAMPLE & GRÀCIA

BA-BA-REEBA

The tapas selection here includes prawns wrapped in bacon and sea urchins filled with melted cheese.

Passeig de Gràcia 28 93 301 43 02 Passeig de Gràcia

LA BODEGUETA

An old wine tavern, well known for its *charcuterie* and local wines and vermouths.

Rambla de Catalunya 100 93 215 48 94 Closed Sun lunch Provença

CIUDAT CONDAL CERVECERIA

A popular meeting-place in the centre of town for breakfast or coffee.

Rambla de Catalunya 18 93 318 19 97 Catalunya

FLASH-FLASH TORTILLERIA (€)

The place for cheap, healthy Spanish fast food – *tortillas* (omelettes) and salad.

Carrer Granada del Penedes 25 93 237 09 90 Diagonal

PLA DE LA GARSA

A former 16th-century stables and dairy near the Picasso Museum now a beautiful bar-restaurant, known for its cheeses, pâtés and hams.

Carrer Assaonadors 13 · 93 315 24 13

Closed lunch · Jaume I

QU-QU (QUASI QUEVIURES)

A delicatessen-cum-tapas bar, specialising in salads, cheeses and Catalan sausage meats.

Passeig de Gràcia 24 · 93 317 45 12

Passeig de Gràcia

TAPA TAPA

The place to meet for tapas and a beer. Specials include snails, fried pig snout, black squid and octopus.

Passeig de Gràcia 44 · 93 488 33 69

Passeig de Gràcia

Where to stay Barcelona

ARTS BARCELONA (€€€)

Barcelona's most fashionable hotel provides state-of-the-art, unabashed luxury beside the sea.

www.ritzcarlton.com

✉ Carrer de la Marina 19–21 ☎ 93 221 10 00 🚇 Ciutadella/Vila Olímpica

BARCELONA HILTON (€€€)

High-amenity hotel, 15 minutes from the airport, at the heart of the city's com-mercial and financial district.

www.hilton.com

✉ Avinguda Diagonal 589–591 ☎ 93 495 77 77 🚇 Maria Cristina

CITADINES (€€)

A 3-star 'aparthotel' on the Ramblas, with a rooftop terrace overlooking part of the Old City.

www.citadines.com

✉ La Rambla 122 ☎ 93 270 11 11 Ⓜ Catalunya/Liceu

CLARIS (€€€)

Just off the exclusive Passeig de Gràcia, this impressive hotel features modern accommodation furnished in marble, glass and works of art. Several restaurants, a roof terrace with pool, a fitness centre, a Japanese garden and even a museum of priceless Egyptian antiques.

www.derbyhotels.es

✉ Carrer Pau Claris 150 ☎ 93 487 62 62 Ⓜ Passeig de Gràcia

COLÓN (€€–€€€)

Old-fashioned, family-friendly hotel, opposite the cathedral. Country-home feel rather than that of a busy city hotel.

www.hotelcolon.es

✉ Avenida de la Catedral 7 ☎ 93 301 14 04 Ⓜ Jaume I/ Urquinaona

CONDES DE BARCELONA (€€€)

Stylish hotel in Barcelona's main shopping district. Elegant public rooms, and bedrooms furnished in *Modernista* style.

www.condesdebarcelona.es

Passeig de Gràcia 73–75 93 467 47 80 Diagonal

DUQUES DE BERGARA (€€)

Contemporary elegance in a turn-of-the-19th-century building. Four stars.

www.hoteles-catalonia.es

Carrer Bergara 11 93 301 51 51 Catalunya

GALLERY (€€€)

You'll get a warm welcome and relaxing stay at this lovely hotel. Ask for their leaflet with five city strolls.

www.galleryhotel.com

Carrer Roselló 249 93 415 99 11 Diagonal

GAUDÍ (€€)

Facing Palau Güell, one of Gaudí's masterworks, this modern 3-star hotel has 73 well-equipped rooms and a Gaudí-inspired reception area.

www.hotelgaudi.es

✉ Carrer Nou de la Rambla 12 ☎ 93 317 90 32 Ⓜ Drassanes/Liceu

GRAN HOTEL BARCINO (€€€)

Modern luxury and tasteful rooms await you here in the heart of the Barri Gòtic.

www.gargallo-hotels.com

✉ Carrer Jaume I, 6 ☎ 93 302 20 12; Ⓜ Jaume I

GRAN VÍA (€)

It is easy to imagine how splendid this reasonably priced hotel must have been in its heyday, with its old-world gilt, balustraded staircase and chandeliers.

www.nnhotels.es

✉ Gran Via de les Cortes Catalanes 642 ☎ 93 318 19 00

Ⓜ Catalunya

GRAVINA (€€)

This charming 3-star hotel has a prime location near the bustling Plaça de Catalunya.

www.hotel-gravina.com

✉ Carrer Gravina 12 ☎ 93 301 68 68 Ⓜ Universitat

JARDÍ (€)

A small, friendly hotel with clean, simple rooms overlooking two of the Barri Gòtic's prettiest squares, Plaça Sant Josep Oriol and Plaça del Pi.

✉ Plaça Sant Josep Oriol 1 ☎ 93 301 59 00 🚇 Liceu

MÉSON CASTILLA (€)

A quiet, characterful family-run hotel on the edge of the old town, with 56 rooms furnished in traditional style.

www.mesoncastilla.com

✉ Carrer Valldonzella 5 ☎ 93 318 21 82 🚇 Universitat

ORIENTE (€€)

The Oriente was once the place to stay in Barcelona. Restored but still traditionally furnished, it draws those seeking a taste of history.

www.husa.es

✉ La Rambla 45 ☎ 93 302 25 58 🚇 Liceu

REY JUAN CARLOS I CONRAD INTERNATIONAL (€€€)

A member of the 'Leading Hotels of the World' group, set in private gardens and with extensive views of the city. First-rate facilities.

www.hrjuancarlos.com

✉ Avinguda Diagonal 661–671 ☎ 93 364 40 40 Ⓜ Zona Universitària

RIALTO (€)

The cosy atmosphere and bedrooms stylishly furnished with Catalan flair makes this 3-star hotel in the Barri Gòtic an excellent choice.

www.gargallo-hotels.com

✉ Carrer Ferran 42 ☎ 93 318 52 12 Ⓜ Jaume I

RITZ (€€€)

Part of the 'Leading Hotels ofthe World' group, this hotel has gracious old-world charm, solicitous staff and a reputation for excellent cuisine and service.

www.rtizbcn.com

✉ Gran Via de les Corts Catalanes 668 ☎ 93 510 1130
Ⓜ Passeig de Gràcia

RIVOLI RAMBLA (€€€)

Opened in 1989, this hotel immediately established itself as one of the best. Behind the dignified *Modernista* façade, the interior contains murals, art deco furnishings and many antiques. A rooftop terrace overlooks the smarter end of La Rambla.

www.rivolihotels.com

✉ La Rambla 128 ☎ 93 302 66 43 Ⓜ Catalunya

ROMA REIAL (€)

Excellent, cheap accommodation overlooking the Plaça Reial. Service is friendly and all rooms have bathroom and phone.

✉ Plaça Reial 11 ☎ 93 302 03 66 Ⓜ Liceu

SANT AGUSTÍ (€)

Just off La Rambla, and near Boqueria market, this smart, modern 3-star hotel offers excellent value in a quiet yet central location.

www.hotelsa.com

✉ Plaça Sant Agustí 3 ☎ 93 318 16 58 Ⓜ Liceu

Exploring Catalonia

It would be a shame to visit Barcelona without also seeing something of Catalunya (Catalonia). Despite being an autonomous province of Spain, this unique region feels in many ways like a separate country, with its own language and deeply rooted traditions, culture and cuisine. Its geographical location makes it the gateway to Spain. Over the centuries the passage of many peoples and civilisations has shaped the region, leaving magical cities such as Girona and Tarragona brimming with historical monuments, while its beautiful landscapes have provided inspiration for such artists as Gaudí, Miró, Dalí and Picasso.

The Catalan landscape is easy to tour, and offers a wide variety of scenery, from the dramatic, snow-capped peaks of the Pyrenees and the secret bays and bustling fishing ports of the Costa Brava, north of Barcelona, to the acclaimed Penedès vineyards and golden beaches of the Costa Daurada to the south.

FIGUERES

The main claim to fame of Figueres, two hours' drive northwest of Barcelona and just 17km from the Franco-Spanish border, is that the great Surrealist painter Salvador Dalí was born here in 1904 and gave his first exhibition in the town

when he was just 14. In 1974, he inaugurated his remarkable **Teatre-Museu Dalí** and to this day it remains the most visited museum in Spain after the Prado in Madrid.

The building, topped with a massive metallic dome and decorated with egg shapes, is original and spectacular – in keeping with Dalí's powerful personality. Its galleries are housed in enclosed, circular tiers around a central stage and a courtyard containing a 'Rainy Taxi' and a tower of car tyres crowned by a boat and an umbrella. The galleries contain paintings, sculptures, jewellery, drawings and other works from Dalí's private collection along with weird and wonderful constructions from different periods of his career, including a bed with fish tails, skeletal figures and a life-sized orchestra. Dalí died in Figueres in 1989, leaving his estate to the Spanish state. His body lies behind a granite slab inside the museum.

Other sights in Figueres include the Museu de Juguets (Toy Museum) and the Museu de l'Empordà (Art and History).

Plaça del Sol 972 50 31 55 Plenty (€–€€)
Teatre-Museu Dalí Plaça Gala-Salvador Dalí 5 972 67 75 00 Oct–Jun Tue–Sat 10:30–5:45; Jul–Sep daily 9–7:45. Closed 1 Jan and 25 Dec None Very expensive

MONTSERRAT

Fifty-six kilometres northwest of Barcelona, at the summit of Catalonia's 1,200m-high holy mountain, Montserrat is one of the most important pilgrimage sites in the whole of Spain. Thousands travel here every year to venerate a medieval statue of the Madonna and Child called *La Moreneta* (The Black Virgin), blackened by the smoke of millions of candles over the centuries. The statue is said to have been made by St Luke and brought to the area by St Peter, and is displayed above the altar of the monastery church.

The spectacularly sited monastery, founded in 1025, is also famous for its choir, La Escolania, one of the oldest and best-known boys' choirs in Europe. The choir sings daily at 1pm in the Basilica, a striking edifice containing important paintings including works by El Greco and Caravaggio.

Montserrat is clearly signposted by road from Barcelona, although the most enjoyable way to get there is by FGC train from Plaça d'Espanya, followed by a thrilling cable-car ride up to the monastery.

Plaça de la Creu, Montserrat ☎ 93 877 77 77 Limited choice of bars and restaurants

GIRONA

Just 1.5 hours by car or train from Barcelona, the beautiful, walled city of Girona is one of Catalonia's most characterful cities, with an admirable collection of ancient monuments. The old city, built on a steep hill and known for its lovely stairways, arcaded streets and sunless alleys, is separated from modern Girona by the River Onyar. The medieval, multicoloured houses overhanging the river are a photographer's dream, especially when seen from the iron footbridge designed by Eiffel. Most of the main sights are in the old city. Make sure you allow plenty of time to shop along the beautiful

Rambla de la Llibertat and to stop and enjoy a drink and people-watch in the arcaded Plaça de la Independencia.

At the heart of the old city, centred around Carrer de la Força, El Call, the old Jewish quarter, is one of the best preserved in Western Europe and is particularly atmospheric by night, with its street lanterns and intimate restaurants. Another splendid sight is the **Catedral**, with its impressive staircase leading up to a fine baroque façade, a magnificent medieval interior and the widest Gothic vault in Europe. Housed inside another church, the Museu Arqueològic (Archaeological Musuem) outlines the city's history, and provides access to the Passeig Arqueològic, a panoramic walk around the walls of the old city. Near by, the 13th-century Banys Arabs (Arab Bath-house), probably designed by Moorish craftsmen following the Moors' occupation of Girona, is the best preserved of its kind in Spain after the Alhambra, particularly striking for its fusion of Arab and Romanesque styles.

Rambla de la Llibertat 1 972 22 65 75 Plenty (€–€€)
Catedral Plaça de la Catedral 972 21 44 26 Tue–Sat 10–2, 4–7, Sun 10–2 Good Free

PENEDÈS WINERIES – VILAFRANCA AND SANT SADURNÍ D'ANOIA

The Alt Penedès is one of Spain's most respected wine-producing areas, producing Catalonia's best-known wines and all of its *cava* (sparkling wine). Since ancient times, viticulture has been the main economic activity of its two main towns, Sant Sadurní d'Anoia and Vilafranca del Penedès.

Only half an hour's drive from Barcelona, Sant Sadurní is the centre of Catalonia's *cava* industry, with 66 *cava* firms in the town. The largest, Codorniu, produces around 40 million bottles a year and its magnificent *Modernista* plant is open to visitors daily. Tours last 1.5 hours and include a tasting.

Near by, Vilafranca del Penedès, the region's capital town, has more character than Sant Sadurní, with its fine arcaded streets and medieval mansions. In the Gothic quarter, surrounded by squares, palaces and churches, the **Museu del Vi** is the only museum in Catalonia to be wholly dedicated to wine. Current methods of production can be observed at Vilafranca's three top wineries – **Mas Tinell**, **Romagosa Torné** and **Miguel Torres** – all located just outside the town centre on the BP2121 to Sant Martí Sarroca.

Museu del Vi ✉ Plaça Jaume I, 1 and 3, Vilafranca del Penedès
☎ 93 890 05 82 ⏲ Jun–Aug Tue–Sat 10–9, Sun 10–2; Sep–May Tue–Sat 10–2, 4–7, Sun 10–2 ✋ Cheap

Penedès Wineries ☎ Codorníu: 93 818 32 32; Caves Romagosa Torné: 93 899 13 53; Mas Tinell: 93 817 05 86; Miguel Torres: 93 817 74 00 ⏲ Opening times vary. Phone individual wineries for details

SITGES

Sitges, 40km south of Barcelona, is one of Spain's oldest bathing resorts and has long been the weekend and holiday playground of Barcelonans. It was once a sleepy fishing port and, although it has now developed into a thriving seaside destination, the old town still retains its ancient charm, with narrow streets, whitewashed cottages and flower-festooned balconies. It also has several appealing *Modernista* buildings.

It was artist and writer Santiago Rusinyol who first put Sitges on the map, bringing it to the attention of artists such as Manuel de Falla, Ramon Casas, Nonell, Utrillo and Picasso. Rusinyol's house, Cau Ferrat, is today a museum, containing works by El Greco and Picasso amongst others. Neighbouring Museu Maricel de Mar houses an interesting collection of medieval and baroque artefacts, including Catalan ceramics, and the nearby Museu Romántic provides a fascinating insight into 18th-century patrician life in Sitges.

Sitges is famous for its beautiful Platja d'Or (Golden Beach), which stretches southwards for 5km. Its promenade is dotted with beach bars, cafés and fine fish restaurants. However, the resort is perhaps best-known for its vibrant nightlife, drawing a young crowd throughout the summer. It is also a popular gay holiday destination. From October to May, Sitges is quieter, except during *Carnaval* in mid-February when the town comes alive with parties and parades, drawing spectators from afar.

i Carrer Sinia Morera 1 ☎ 93 93 894 50 04/93 894 42 51
🍴 Plenty (€–€€)

drive

The main attraction of this drive is its magnificent scenery. Leave Vilafranca del Penedès on the BP2121 past Mas Tinell, Romagosa Torné and Torres wineries (➤ 172), until you reach Sant Martí Sarroca after 9km.

This agricultural village contains an important Romanesque church with a splendid Gothic altarpiece, and a 9th-century castle.

Continue on to Torrelles de Foix, with its tiled church dome. The road then climbs through barren scrub up to Pontons. Continue up past the Romanesque church of Valldossera, through Els Ranxox, over the Coll de la Torreta, to Santes Creus.

Santes Creus, founded in 1158 alongside the Gaia river, is one of three exceptional former Cistercian monasteries in the region (the others are Poblet and Vallbona de les Monges). Following its deconsecration, it grew into a small village in 1843 when a group of families moved into the abandoned buildings and monks' residences.

Turn right at the main road (TP2002) to El Pont d'Armentera. Join the T213 to Igualada. After 22km of breathtaking mountain scenery, turn right to La Llacuna, then left through farmland to Mediona. Continue to St Pere Sacarrera then turn right at the main road to St Quinti de Mediona. Several kilometres later, turn left to Sant Pere de Riudebitlles.

Mediona is noted for its medieval church and ruined castle, while St Pere de Riudebitlles boasts a splendid Gothic manor house – the Palace of the Marquis of Lo.

*The same road eventually leads to Sant Sadurní (**➤ 176**).*

Distance 105km **Time** 3–3.5 hours (without stops) **Start point** Vilafranca del Penedès **End point** Sant Sadurní d'Anoia

Lunch break 🍴 Sant Jordi/Ca La Katy (€€) ✉ 81/2 km outside Vilafranca del Penedès ☎ 93 899 13 26

Vilafranca del Penedès ℹ Carrer Cort 14 ☎ 93 818 12 54 🍴 Plenty (€–€€)

Sant Martí Sarroca ℹ Plaça de l'Ajuntament 1 ☎ 93 891 31 88 🍴 Limited choice (€€)

TARRAGONA

This agreeable city is surprisingly undiscovered by most foreign visitors to the region, even though it contains the largest ensemble of Roman remains in Spain, the remarkable architectural legacy of Roman Tarraco, capital of an area that once covered half the Iberian peninsula. Originally settled by Iberians and then Carthaginians, it later became the base for the Roman conquest of Spain and the main commercial centre on this stretch of the coast until Barcelona and Valencia overshadowed it, after the Christian re-conquest of Spain in the early 12th century.

The town is sited on a rocky hill, sloping down to the sea. The ancient upper town contains most of the Roman ruins, some museums and an attractive medieval quarter with a grand cathedral. Below the Old Town lies the modern shopping district, centred on the Rambla Nova with its smart boutiques and restaurants, and a daily fruit and vegetable market in Plaça Corsini. Below the main town, the chief attraction of the lower part of the city is the maritime district of El Serrallo with its colourful fishing fleet, traditional *Lonja* (fish auction), and dockside restaurants that serve fish fresh from the nets. The rocky coastline beyond conceals a couple of beaches, notably Platja Arrabassada and Platja Llarga.

DISCOVER TARRAGONA

AMFITEATRE ROMA

Built into the hillside overlooking the Mediterranean, the Amfiteatre Roma (Roman Amphitheatre) was where the Romans held their public spectacles, including combats between gladiators and wild animals before an audience of some 12,000 people. During the 12th century the Romanesque church of Santa Maria del Miracle was built on the site, giving the beach below its name – El Miracle. You can visit the Amfiteatre, Passeig Arqueològic, Museu d'Història, Circ Romà (➤ 182) and Casa Museu de Castellarnau (➤ 190) on a combined ticket.

✉ Carrer Oleguer ☎ 977 24 25 79 🕔 Tue–Sat Apr–Jun 10–1.30, 3.30–6.30; Jul–Sep 9–9; Oct–Mar 10.30–1.30, 3.30–5.30. Closed Mon. Sun Summer 9–3; Winter 10–2 ♿ None 🎫 Moderate (combined ticket)

CATEDRAL

Tarragona's grandiose Catedral – a magnificent Romanesque-Gothic building, in the form of a cross – was built as the centrepiece of the *ciutat antigua* (old city).

✉ Plaça de la Seu ☎ 977 23 86 85 🕒 Mon–Sat 10–1, 4–7; winter 10–2

MUSEU ARQUEOLÒGIC AND MUSEU D'HISTÒRIA

The fascinating Museu Arqueològic (Archeological Museum) includes a section of the old Roman wall, statues of emperors, several sarcophagi and some interesting mosaics. Near by stands the Praetorium and the vaults of the 1st-century Roman Circus. The Praetorium is the site of the Museu d'Història (Tarragona History Museum), which traces the origins and history of the city through such treasures as the sarcophagus of Hipolitus, a masterpiece that was rescued from the sea in 1948.

✉ Plaça del Rei ☎ 977 23 62 09 🕒 Museu Arqueològic: Tue–Sat 10–1, 4.30–7 (8 in summer), Sun 11–2. Museu d'Història: Tue–Sat 10–5.30, Sun 10–3 ✋ Moderate (combined ticket)

drive

The Costa Daurada (Golden Coast) takes its name from its long sandy beaches. This short drive starts in Tarragona and covers its northernmost stretch.

Leave Tarragona on the N340 coast road towards Barcelona. A few kilometres later you will arrive at the resorts of Altafulla and Torredembarra.

These two thriving holiday resorts attained great prosperity in the 18th century as a result of the wine trade with the American colonies. Note the Renaissance-style castle at Torredembarra.

Continue on the N340 for 6km. Turn left to Creixell.

The hilltop village of Creixell boasts a ruined medieval castle and a church with a striking Modernista belltower.

Return to the N340. After 2km, the road skirts the 2nd-century Roman Arc de Bara then continues to Coma-Ruga and Sant Salvador.

Coma-Ruga was once an area of marshland with

mineral-water springs. At the turn of the 19th century two spas were established around which this bustling resort developed. The local speciality, *xató* – a scrumptious cold fish salad, with a dressing similar to *romesco* – must be sampled. At Sant Salvador, the cellist Pau Casals had his summer residence; today it is a museum.

From the Museu Pau Casals, the coast road leads to Calafell, where fishing boats are launched straight from the sand. Join the N246 here (direction Barcelona) and follow signs to Vilanova i la Geltrú.

The busy commercial centre of Vilanova is also a popular resort, thanks to its sandy beach, its palm-lined seafront, and its many appealing restaurants.

Continue on the N246 to Sitges (➤ 174).

Distance 63km **Time** 1 hour (without stops) **Start point** Tarragona **End point** Sitges **Lunch break** 🍴 Casa Victor (€€) ✉ Passeig Maritim 23, Coma-Ruga ☎ 977 68 14 73

MUSEU I NECROPOLIA PALEOCRISTIANS

Tarragona's most treasured Roman remains are housed in the Museu i Necropolia Paleocristians (Paleo-Christian Museum), in what was once an ancient necropolis, a 20-minute walk west of the city centre. It includes a valuable collection of mosaics, pottery, metalwork, glass and ivory.

Passeig de la Independència s/n 977 21 11 75
Seasonal variations. Call for times Moderate

PASSEIG ARQUEOLÒGIC

For an overview of the old city and the flat hinterland of the Camp de Tarragona, walk the Passeig Arqueològic, a promenade which encircles the northernmost half of the old town, around the Roman walls, of which 1km of the original 4km remains. Seven defence towers and gates still stand, giving access to the city.

Passeig Arqueològic 977 24 57 96 As for Amfiteatre Roma Moderate

walk

Start in Plaça de la Font. Take Carrer del Cós del Bou, at the opposite end to the Ajuntament building, up to the Circ Romà.

These ruins are all that remain of Tarragona's Roman Circus, which once occupied the Plaça de la Font.

Continue up Baixada de la Peixateria, turn right into Carrer de l'Enrajolat and immediately left into Plaça del Rei.

The Museu Arqueològic and the Museu d'Història (► 182) provide a useful overview of the early history of Tarragona.

A small unmarked street beside the Museu Arqueològic leads to Plaça dels Angels. From here go left, then first right along Carrer Santa Anna as far as Plaça del Forum.

Of particular interest here is a section of wall and the ruins of the Roman Forum, currently under excavation.

*Take Carrer Merceria past the Gothic arches, then climb the steps to the Catedral (**➤ 182**). Circle this magnificent building anticlockwise. In Plaça de Palau, steps lead down to Carrer Claustre and the entrance to the Cathedral and the cloister.*

The medieval cloisters here, bathed in light filtered through arches and trees, provide a retreat from the city.

Return to Plaça de Palau. Turn left down Carrer de la Guitarra, through Plaça Sant Joan, along Baixada del Roser (alongside the old city wall) and left into Plaça del Paillol. Follow the road round into Carrer dels Cavalers past Casa Castellarnau (one of Tarragona's finest medieval mansions). A right turn into Carrer Major swings round into Baixada Misericordia and brings you back to the main square, Plaça de la Font.

Distance 1.5 km **Time** 1 hour (without visits)
Start/end point Ajuntament, Plaça de la Font **Coffee-break** Can Peret (€) Plaça de la Font 6 977 23 76 25

Where to eat & drink... Catalonia

RESTAURANTS & CAFÉS/BARS

GIRONA

L'ARCADA (€)

Chic café bar-cum-restaurant underneath Rambla Llibertat's handsome arcade.

✉ Rambla Llibertat 38 ☎ 972 20 10 15

CIPRESAIA (€€)

Smart, sophisticated restaurant, at the heart of the old Jewish quarter.

Carrer General Fornas 2 · 972 22 24 49 · Closed Thu

EL POU DE CALL (€€)

Local cuisine in traditional surroundings. Excellent-value *menú del diá* and wine list.

Carrer de la Força 14 · 972 22 37 74 · Closed Sun eve

MONTSERRAT

ABAT CISNEROS (€€)

Montserrat's top restaurant. The 16th-century stone dining-room used to contain the monastery stables.

Hotel Abat Cisneros · 93 877 77 01

SITGES

CHIRINGUITO (€)

A traditional-style tapas bar in a wooden hut on the seafront, specialising in fresh sardines and salads

Passeig de la Ribera · 93 894 75 96

MARE NOSTRUM (€€)

Smart waterfront restaurant. Try the *xato de Sitges* (grilled fish with a local variant of *romesco* sauce, ➤ 53), or monkfish and prawns with garlic mousseline.

✉ Passeig de la Ribera 60–62 ☎ 93 894 33 93 ⌚ Closed Wed & mid-Dec to end Jan

TARRAGONA

BODEGA CELLER GRAS (€)

A good place to join the locals for tapas specialities – pâtés, cheeses and *charcuterie*, including spicy *xoriço* and Mallorquin *sobrassada*.

✉ Carrer Governadir Gonzalez 8 ☎ 977 23 48 20
⌚ Closed Sun eve

BUFET EL TIBERI (€–€€)

Kitsch but fun, this Catalan theme restaurant comes complete with staff in traditional dress. The food is unexceptional but is a good bet for travellers on a budget.

Carrer Martí d'Ardenya 5 ☎ 977 23 54 03 ⌚ Closed Sun eve, Mon

ESTACIÓ MARITIMA (€€€)

This is one of the best of the many fish restaurants and tapas bars that line the waterfront in the fishermen's district of Serralló.

✉ Moll de Costa Tinglade 4 ☎ 977 22 74 18 🕒 Closed Sun eve and Mon

SOL-RIC (€€)

Excellent fish restaurant located on the outskirts of town near Platja Rembassada.

✉ Via Augusta 227 ☎ 977 23 20 32 🕒 Closed Mon eve, Sun

VILAFRANCA DEL PENEDÈS

CAL TON (€€)

It may come as a surprise to find such a smart, modern restaurant in an otherwise traditional town. Try the mouth-watering pancakes filled with a seafood and *cava* sauce.

✉ Carrer del Casal 8 ☎ 93 890 37 41 🕒 Closed Sun eve and Mon, Easter week, 2 Aug

Where to stay... Catalonia

FIGUERES

HOTEL DURÁN (€€)

This popular hotel also has a highly regarded restaurant, that serves hearty traditional cuisine with a modern touch. Was a favourite haunt of Salvador Dalí and friends.

www.hotelduran.com ✉ Carrer Lasuaca 5 ☎ 972 50 12 50

GIRONA

BELLMIRALL (€)

Characterful hotel, housed inside the ancient buildings of the Jewish quarter and near to the cathedral. Feels more like a country dwelling.

✉ Carrer Bellmirall 3 ☎ 972 20 40 09

CARLEMANY (€€€)

Smart, modern hotel between the station and the old town, full of modern art. Its restaurant is one of the best in town.

www.carlemany.es ✉ Plaça Miquel Santaló ☎ 972 21 12 12

MONTSERRAT

CAPRI-VERACRUZ (€–€€)

Excellent value just off the seafront, this family-run hotel consists of two houses with an outdoor pool and terrace.

✉ Avinguda Sofia 13–17 ☎ 93 811 02 67

EL XALET (€)

A discreet hotel in a beautiful Modernista villa, with just 10 well-furnished rooms, restaurant, pool and garden.

✉ Carrer Isla de Cuba 35 ☎ 93 811 0070

TARRAGONA

FÒRUM (€)

Simple, clean rooms overlooking Plaça de la Font in the Old Town, above a jolly *bodega*-style restaurant.

✉ Plaça de la Font 37 ☎ 977 23 17 18

URBIS (€)

Reasonably priced, friendly 3-star hotel in the town centre, just off the Rambla Nova and near the daily fruit market.

✉ Carrer Reding 20 bis ☎ 977 24 01 16

shopping & leisure

SHOPPING

CLOTHES, JEWELLERY & ACCESSORIES

ADOLFO DOMÍNGUEZ

One of Spain's most famous designers, Adolfo Domínguez is renowned for introducing linen suits in the 1980s with the slogan 'wrinkles are fashionable'. He also designed this shop.

✉ Passeig de Gràcia 32 ☎ 93 487 41 70 Ⓜ Passeig de Gràcia

ALEA

Splendid showcase for up-and-coming Catalan jewellers in the newly trendy district of La Ribera.

✉ Carrer Argenteria 66 ☎ 93 310 13 73 Ⓜ Jaume I, Barceloneta

ANTONIO MIRÓ

Antonio Miró is Spain's brightest young fashion star. Although best known for his men's fashions, he also designs women's and children's clothes, shoes, spectacles and furniture.

✉ Carrer Consell de Cent 349–351 ☎ 93 487 06 70 Ⓜ Passeig de Gràcia

0,925 ARGENTERS

Small, chic jewellery shop near the Picasso Museum featuring work in gold, silver, platinum and steel from four young Spanish designers.

✉ Carrer Montcada 25 ☎ 93 319 43 18 🚇 Jaume I

BAGUÉS

This shop on the ground floor of Casa Amatller contains priceless works by Masriera, the sole creator of the *Modernista* style in the Spanish jewellery trade.

✉ Passeig de Gràcia 41 ☎ 93 216 01 73 🚇 Passeig de Gràcia

BÓBOLI

A leading Spanish brand for children and teens clothing. Comfortable, stylish and sporty.

✉ Carrer Gran de Gràcia 98 ☎ 93 237 56 70 🚇 Gràcia

CARLES GALINDO

Stylish shop-cum-showroom featuring local designer Carles Galindo's collection of accessories for both sexes – handbags, belts and jewellery often made from unusual materials.

✉ Carrer Verdi 56 ☎ 93 416 07 04 Ⓜ Lesseps

CRISTINA CASTANER

All the latest trends in women's footwear, plus handbags and other accessories.

✉ Carrer Mestre Nicolau 23 ☎ 93 414 24 28 Ⓜ Maria Cristina, Hospital Clínic

JOAQUÍN BERAO

Jewellery by Joaquín Berao, celebrated for his unusual combinations of materials and avant-garde chunky designs.

✉ Rambla de Catalunya 74 ☎ 93 215 00 91 Ⓜ Diagonal

LYDIA DELGADO

Delgado is one of Barcelona's most distinctive local designers of easy-to-wear women's fashions. Her collections are sold in this shop alone.

✉ Carrer Minerva 21 ☎ 93 415 99 98 Ⓜ Gràcia, Diagonal

LOEWE

One of the most celebrated leather-goods companies in the world, located in Domènech i Montaner's *Modernista* Lleó-Morera building.

✉ Passeig de Gràcia 35 ☎ 93 216 04 00 Ⓜ Passeig de Gràcia

MANGO

This chainstore brims with affordable, trendy designs. Several branches around Barcelona, include a large one at Passeig de Gràcia 65 and another inside the L'Illa Diagonal shopping mall.

✉ Avinguda Portal de l'Àngel 7 ☎ 93 317 69 85 Ⓜ Catalunya

LA MANUAL ALPARGATERA

This shop has been making traditional Spanish espadrilles by hand since 1910.

✉ Carrer Avinyó 7 ☎ 93 301 01 72 Ⓜ Jaume I, Liceu

MUXART CHIC

This is a vibrant shop showcasing shoes by Barcelonan shoe designer, Muxart.

✉ Carrer Roselló 230 ☎ 93 488 10 64 Ⓜ Provença, Diagonal B
Rambla Catalunya 47 Ⓜ Catalunya

NOEL BARCELONA

All the latest trends in footwear, from thigh boots to not-very-sensible-but-fun platform trainers.

✉ Carrer Pelai 46 ☎ 93 317 86 38 Ⓜ Catalunya, Universitat

PEDRO ALONSO

This small shop with its gloves, fans and imitation jewellery, once catered mainly for stage performers, but today has a more diverse clientele.

✉ Carrer Santa Anna 27 ☎ 93 317 60 85 Ⓜ Catalunya

SOLE

Shoes, boots and sandals made of fine Moroccan and Spanish leather, including Spanish cowboy boots.

✉ Carrer Ample 7 ☎ 93 301 69 84 Ⓜ Drassnes

ZARA

A nationwide chain of trendy fashion stores, popular with young shoppers.

✉ Carrer Pelai 58 ☎ 93 301 09 78 Ⓜ Catalunya

ART, CRAFTS, GIFTS & DESIGN

AJUPA'T

A veritable treasure trove of original gift ideas, including chunky local jewellery, handicrafts, papier mâché and paper goods.

✉ Carrer València 261 ☎ 93 488 24 13 Ⓜ Passeig de Gràcia

ART ESCUDELLERS

Huge emporium selling Spanish pottery and ceramics, from factory pieces to arty individual designs. Basement wine cellar, delicatessen and wine bar.

✉ Carrer Escudellers 23 ☎ 93 412 68 01 🕐 Daily 11–11 Ⓜ Liceu, Drassanes

ATALANTA MANUFACTURA

Just behind Santa Maria del Mar, a husband-and-wife team from Madrid paint beautiful silk scarves, often inspired by local art and architecture. Personalised designs upon request.

✉ Passeig del Born 10 ☎ 93 268 37 02 Ⓜ Jaume 1

BARAKA

A treasure trove of Moroccan souvenirs with a wide range of gift ideas from hookah pipes and incense, to jewellery and mirrored, embroidered blouses.

✉ Carrer Canvis Vells 2 ☎ 93 268 42 20 Ⓜ Jaume 1

BD EDICIONES DE DISENO

Winner of several awards for its state-of-the-art furniture and household design, beautifully displayed in a striking *Modernista* house by Domènech i Montaner.

✉ Carrer Mallorca 291 ☎ 93 458 69 09 Ⓜ Diagonal

CENTRE CATAL D'ARTESANIA

Impressive centre of Catalan handicrafts contains fine ceramics, jewellery, textiles, sculptures and glassware of the region.

✉ Passeig de Gràcia 55 ☎ 93 467 46 60 Ⓜ Passeig de Gràcia

CERERIA SUBIRÀ

The oldest shop in the city, founded in 1761, selling candles ancient and modern, religious and profane.

✉ Baixada Llibreteria 7

☎ 93 315 26 06 Ⓜ Jaume I

COSES DE CASA

Handmade patchwork quilts and fabrics, including the distinctive Mallorcan *roba de llengües* (literally 'cloth of tongues'), striking for its red, blue or green zigzag patterns.

✉ Plaça Sant Josep Oriol 5 ☎ 93 302 73 28 Ⓜ Jaume I

GERMANES GARCIA

Wickerwork of all shapes and sizes tumbles out of this village-style shop into the streets of the Old City.

✉ Carrer Banys Nous 15 ☎ 93 318 66 46 Ⓜ Liceu

ICI ET LA

Interesting, exotic shop stocking new furniture, lighting and accessories by young Spanish designers.

✉ Plaça Santa Maria del Mar 2 ☎ 93 268 11 67 Ⓜ Jaume 1

D BARCELONA

A wide choice of gifts and avant-garde household items, together with temporary exhibitions presenting the work of young designers as well as some of the more established names.

✉ Avinguda Diagonal 367 ☎ 93 216 03 46 Ⓜ Diagonal

DOS I UNA

The first design shop in Barcelona – a tiny treasure trove of gadgets and unusual gift ideas.

✉ Carrer Rosselló 275 ☎ 93 217 70 32 Ⓜ Diagonal

GALERIA MAEGHT

Come to these specialists in 20th-century art, design and photography for posters, prints and other graphic works. Upstairs is a prestigious art gallery.

✉ Carrer Montcada 25 ☎ 93 301 42 54 Ⓜ Liceu, Jaume I

LTACA

Folk pottery and crafted glassware from all parts of Spain, Mexico and Morocco.

✉ Carrer Ferran 24–26 ☎ 93 301 30 44 Ⓜ Liceu

LA MANUAL ALPARGATERA

All kinds of handmade, straw woven items, including hats, bags and their speciality, espadrilles.

✉ Carrer Avinyó 7 ☎ 93 301 01 72 Ⓜ Liceu, Jaume I

MUSEU PICASSO

One of Barcelona's many notable museum shops reflecting the city's connections with this major 20th century artist.

✉ Carrer Montcada 15 ☎ 93 319 63 10 Ⓜ Jaume I

POBLE ESPANYOL

More than 60 art and craft shops in a reproduction 'Spanish Village' selling traditional wares from all corners of Spain.

✉ Avinguda del Marqués de Comillas s/n ☎ 93 508 63 00 🚌 13, 61 Ⓜ Espanya

SALA PARÉS

Barcelona's finest gallery – specialises in 19th- and 20th-century paintings, drawings and sculptures.

✉ Carrer Pextritxol 5 ☎ 93 318 70 20 Ⓜ Catalunya

VINÇON

This design 'department store' is Barcelona's answer to Terance Conran. Trendy yet practical household articles at accessible prices. Won the National Design Prize in 1995.

✉ Passeig de Gràcia 96 ☎ 93 215 60 50 Ⓜ Passeig de Gràcia

ANTIQUES, BOOKS & MUSIC

ANGEL BATLLE

Antiquarian books old maps, prints and nautical charts are in abundance here.

Carrer Palla 23 93 301 58 84 Liceu

ARTUR RAMON ANTICUARIO

Two adjacent premises displaying a wide array of antique paintings, sculpture and decorative arts.

Carrer de la Palla 25 93 302 59 70 Jaume I

BULEVARD DELS ANTIQUARIS

Spacious mall containing more than 70 shops for art-lovers and antique collectors. Don't miss Ivan's (93 215 94 09), with its porcelain doll collection, or Turn of the Century (93 215 94 63) for decorative *Modernista* pieces.

Passeig de Gràcia 55 93 215 44 99 Passeig de Gràcia

CASA BEETHOVEN

Founded in 1915, this shop carries scores and sheet music. Specialising in pieces by Spanish and Catalan composers.

La Rambla 97 93 301 48 26 Liceu

CASTELLÓ

Chain of record shops. Carrer Tallers 3 has a huge selection of pop, rock, jazz, blues and soul. No 7 is for classical music.

Carrer Tallers 3 & 7 93 302 59 46 Catalunya

FNAC

A book megastore inside El Triangle shopping mall. Two floors of books, videos, CDs, computers, PlayStations, video games and magazines from all over the world.

Plaça de Catalunya 93 344 18 00 Mon–Sat 10–10
Catalunya

JORDI CAPELL – COOPERATIVE D'ARQUITECTES

Specialist bookshop for architecture and design, in the basement of the College of Architects.

Plaça Nova 5 93 481 35 60 Jaume I, Liceu

LAIE

The best selection of English-language books in Barcelona, including travel maps and guides. Has a café upstairs.

Carrer Pau Claris 85 93 318 17 39 Café: Mon– Sat 9–1
Urquinaona

FOOD & DRINK

BRUNELLS PASTISSERIA

Appears in the *Guinness Book of Records* for making Spain's biggest Easter egg. Try the *torró* (traditional almond fudge), *roques de Montserrat* (meringues) and *carquinyolis* (soft almond biscuits).

✉ Carrer Princesa 22 ☎ 93 319 68 25 Ⓜ Jaume I

CASA GISPERT

Dried fruits, spices, cocoa, coffee, and nuts are toasted daily in a traditional oak-fired oven.

✉ Carrer Sombrerers 23 ☎ 93 319 75 35 Ⓜ Jaume I

COLMADO QUILLEZ

Barcelona's most famous traditional grocery store, selling an array of tinned foods, preserves, cold meats and wines.

✉ Rambla de Catalunya 63 ☎ 93 215 23 56 Ⓜ Passeig de Gràcia

ESCRIBÀ PATISSERIES

Important *Modernista* artists collaborated on the design of this shop. Celebrated for its monumental chocolate cakes.

✉ La Rambla 83 ☎ 93 301 60 27 Ⓜ Liceu

FORMATERÍA CIRERA

A little out of the way but worth a visit, this specialist cheese store sells many unusual Spanish cheeses.

✉ Carrer Cera 45 ☎ 93 441 07 59 Ⓜ Sant Antoni

FORN DE PA SANT JORDI

The long queue outside this bakery is testimony to its excellence. Be sure to taste their *tortellet de cabell d'angel*, a crumbly tart filled with 'angel's hair' (spun candied fruit).

✉ Carrer Llibreteria 8 ☎ 93 310 40 16 Ⓜ Jaume I

MURRIÀ

This *Modernista* store first opened in 1898, and today sells a wide assortment of cheeses, *charcuterie* and other delicacies.

✉ Carrer Roger de Llúria 85 ☎ 93 215 57 89 Ⓜ Passeig de Gràcia

VINS I CAVES LA CATEDRAL

Wines from all over Spain, with a particularly strong selection from Catalonia.

✉ Plaça de Ramon Berenguer el Gran 1 ☎ 93 319 07 27 Ⓜ Jaume I

CHILDREN'S ATTRACTIONS

L'AQUÀRIUM

Barcelona's state-of-the-art aquarium is one of the finest in Europe. As well as the aquatic life on display in 21 tanks, the highlight for most children is the impressive 80m-long tunnel which runs straight through the middle of the shark tank.

✉ Moll d'Espanya, Port Vell ☎ 93 221 74 74 ⌚ Jul–Aug 9.30am–11pm; Jun–Sep & weekends 9:30am–9:30pm; rest of the year 9.30am–9pm ♿ Good 🚇 Barceloneta, Drassanes ✋ Very expensive

BEACHES

Enjoy 4km of clean, sandy beaches with playgrounds, palm-lined promenades and shower facilities. Very good access for people with disabilities.

Platja de Barceloneta, Nova Icària, Bogatell and La Nova Mar Bella
Ciutadella, Selva de Mar

BUS TURÍSTIC

A circuit around the city on the Bus Turístic with 18 stops at key points of interest is an enjoyable way to see the sights. There are two routes, the northern (red) and southern (blue), and you can hop on and off and change routes.

Plaça de Catalunya (or any of its 18 stops) First bus leaves Plaça de Catalunya at 9am Catalunya Tickets for 1 day or 2 days.

ILLA DE FANTASIA

Europe's largest water park is just north of Barcelona on the coast near Mataró. Daily bus from Estació de Sants and Plaça Universitat (93 451 27 72 for bus details).

Carrer Vilassar de Dalt 93 751 45 53 Jun to mid-Sep 10–7
Very expensive

MUSEU DE LA CERA

The Waxwork Museum is ideal for a rainy day. Pinocchio, Superman and other heroes are all here.

Passeig de la Banca, 7 93 317 26 49 Jul–Sep daily 10–10. Oct–Jun Mon–Fri 10–1.30, 4–7.30; weekends & hols 11–2, 4:30–8 Drassanes, Liceu Expensive

MUSEU DEL FUTBOL CLUB BARCELONA

A must for all children who are keen on football at this holiest of shrines to the glorious game.

Nou Camp – Gate 7 or 9 Carrer Arístides Maillol 93 496 36 00 Mon–Sat 10–6.30; Sun and hols 10–2 Café (€)

PARC ZOOLÒGIC

Spain's top zoo boasts over 7,000 animals of 500 different species. There is also a zoo for the under-fives, where children can stroke farm animals and pets, and a dolphinarium which stages spectacular shows (Mon–Fri 11.30, 1.30, 4, Sat, Sun and hols 12, 1.30, 4).

Parc de la Ciutadella 93 225 67 80 Summer daily 9.30am–7.30pm; Winter daily 10–5 Good Ciutadella Very expensive

PORT AVENTURA

Catalonia's answer to Disneyland, and reputedly one of Europe's biggest and best theme parks has been taken over by Universal Studios. Part of the attraction is the introduction of cartoon characters and a ride called *Sea Odyssey*, a graphic simulated underwater journey with computer animation.

✉ Port Aventura, near Salou ☎ 977 77 90 90 ⌚ Mar–Oct Mon–Fri 10–7, Sat and Sun 10–10; mid-June to mid-Sep daily 10–2am ♿ Good 🚆 Port Aventura ✋ Expensive

TIBIDABO AMUSEMENT PARK

Authentic, old-fashioned funfair atmosphere with carousels, bumper cars, a hall of mirrors and a breathtaking open ferris wheel. Getting there, on the ancient Tramvia Blau tramline and then by funicular, is exciting in itself.

✉ Parc d'Atraccions del Tibidabo, Plaça Tibidabo 3–4 ☎ 93 211 79 42 ⌚ Call for opening times. Closed mid-Sep to Mar 🚌 Funicular del Tibidabo ✋ Moderate

NIGHTLIFE

BARS, CLUBS & LIVE MUSIC

BIKINI

One of Barcelona's best night spots, with a popular rock/disco club, a Latin-American salsa room and a classy cocktail lounge.

✉ Carrer Deu i Mata 105 ☎ 93 322 08 00 🕔 Tue–Sat from midnight
🚇 Les Corts, Maria Cristina

LA COVA DEL DRAC

The city's top jazz venue.

✉ Carrer Vallmajor 33 ☎ 93 200 70 32 🕔 Closed Sun and Mon
🚇 Muntaner

DANZATORIA

With its restaurant, disco and beautiful terrace café on the slopes of Tibidabo, this is a favourite summer venue.

✉ Avinguda Tibidabo 61 ☎ 93 206 49 501 🕐 Tue–Sun 7pm–3am 🚇 Tibidabo

ESTADI OLÍMPIC

Main venue for mega-star pop concerts.

✉ Passeig Olímpic ☎ 93 425 49 49 G 61

HARLEM JAZZ CLUB

Small, but very atmospheric jazz club.

✉ Carrer Comtessa de Sobradiel 8 ☎ 93 310 07 55 🕐 Tue–Sun 8pm–4am 🚇 Jaume I

JAMBOREE

A choice nightspot for blues, soul, jazz, funk and occasional hip-hop live bands. Upstairs is Los Tarantos, a laid-back bar.

✉ Plaça Reial ☎ 93 301 75 64 🕐 Daily from 11pm 🚇 Liceu

NAYANDEI BOÎTE

The biggest of the discos on the roof terrace of the

Maremagnum complex. Popular with teenagers.
✉ Maremagnum, Port Vell ☎ 93 225 80 10 🕐 Mon–Sat 9pm–5am, Sun 6pm–5am 🚇 Barceloneta, Drassanes

NICK HAVANNA

One of Barcelona's most talked-about bars, thanks to its sensational design. Go late.
✉ Carrer Rosselló 208 ☎ 93 217 77 32 🕐 Daily 11pm–4am (5am Fri and Sat) 🚇 Diagonal

NITSA

One of the city's best-loved clubs for indie-rock, breakbeat and techno, in a funky dance hall.
✉ Nou de la Rambla 113 ☎ 93 301 00 90 🕐 Fri & Sat, 12.30–6am 🚌 17, 39, 45 57, 59, 64

PASTIS

Small, dimly lit bohemian bar. Sip *pastis* accompanied by Edith Piaf songs played on a phonograph.
✉ Calle Santa Mònica 4 ☎ 93 318 79 80 🕐 Mon, Wed–Sun 7.30pm–2.30am (Fri till 3.30am); closed Tue 🚇 Drassanes

LA TERRAZZA

Summertime open-air club on Montjuïc mountain, behind Poble Espanyol. Gets crowded around 3 or 4am.

Avinguda Marquès de Comilas, Montjuïc 93 423 12 85 Fri–Sat midnight–6am 61

TORRES DE ÁVILA

Trance-techno discos are staged here at weekends and, in summer, the rooftop terrace bars are particularly magical.

Avinguda Marquès de Comillas, Poble Espanyol, Montjuïc 93 424 93 09 Fri, Sat and Sun from 11pm Espanya

UP AND DOWN

Barcelona's most exclusive nightclub.

Carrer Numància 179 93 205 51 94 Disco: Tue–Sat 12am–5.30 or 6am Sants Estació Men must wear a tie

XAMPANYERÍA CASABLANCA

Catalan champagne bar near the Passeig de Gràcia serving four kinds of house cava by the glass as well as tasty tapas.

Carrer Bonavista 6 93 237 63 99 Thu–Sat 8pm–2.30am; (3am Fri & Sat) Passeig de Gràcia

THEATRE, CINEMA, MUSIC & DANCE

AUDITORI

The home of the city's symphony orchestra.

Carrer Lepant 150 93 247 93 00 Marina

CAIXA FORUM

Host to events spanning classical concerts to festivals of poetry.

Aviguda del Marquès de Comillas 6–8 93 476 86 00

Espanya

FILMOTECA DE LA GENERALITAT DE CATALUNYA

Barcelona's official film theatre shows three films a day. These are usually in VO (original version) ie, not in Spanish. There is also a children's programme at 5pm on Sundays.

Cinema Aquitania, Avinguda de Sarrià 31–33 93 410 75 90

Performance: 5, 7.30 and 10pm. Closed hols and Aug

Hospital Clinic

FUNDACIÓ JOAN MIRÓ

Stages a series of concerts (*Nit de Música* – Music Nights) during the summer.

Plaça Neptú, Parc de Montjuïc 93 329 19 08 Jun–Sep 61

GRAN TEATRE DEL LICEU

World-famous singers, including the Catalan diva Montserrat Caballé, have performed here.

✉ La Rambla 51–59 ☎ 93 485 99 13 Ⓜ Liceu

PALAU DE LA MÚSICA CATALÁNA

Barcelona's main venue for classical music (► 98).

✉ Carrer Sant Francesc de Paula 2 ☎ 93 295 72 00 ⏲ Box office: Mon–Fri 10–9; Sat 3–9

EL TABLAO DE CARMEN

Highly rated flamenco cabaret at the Poble Espanyol. Book in advance.

✉ Carrer Arcs 9, Poble Espanyol, Montjuïc ☎ 93 425 46 16 ⏲ Tue–Sun 8pm–1am (2–3am at weekends) ❓ Shows Tue–Sun 9.30. Also 11.30pm on Sat and Sun

TEATRE NACIONAL DE CATALUNYA

This theatre is a showcase for contemporary Catalan dance.

✉ Plaça de les Arts 1 ☎ 93 306 57 00 Ⓜ Glòries

SPORT

SPECTATOR SPORTS

AMERICAN FOOTBALL

ESTADI OLÍMPIC

The 'Barcelona Dragons' play against other teams in the World League on Sundays, April–June. Buy tickets on the day at the stadium.

Passeig Olímpic 17–19 93 425 49 49 61

BASKETBALL

JOVENTUT

League games on Sunday evenings, and European and Spanish Cup matches midweek, September–May. Book tickets in advance.

Avinguda Alfons XIII-Carrer Ponent 143–161, Badalona 93 460 20 40 Gorg

BULLFIGHTING

PLAÇA DE TOROS MONUMENTAL

Barcelona's main bullring and its museum (➤ 90) are open only during the bullfighting season (Apr–Sep). Reserve tickets in advance (☎ 93 453 38 21).

✉ Grand Via de les Corts Catalanes 749 ☎ 93 245 58 04

Ⓜ Monumental

FOOTBALL

NOU CAMP – FC BARCELONA

No visit to Barcelona is complete without a visit to Nou Camp, Europe's largest stadium (seating 120,000), and its museum under the terraces.

✉ Avinguda Aristides Maillol. Museum: Gate 7 or 9 ☎ 93 496 36 00

Ⓜ Collblanc, Maria Cristina

ICE HOCKEY

FC BARCELONA PISTA DE GEL

Barcelona's only professional ice-hockey team. On non-match days, the rink is open to the public.

✉ Avinguda de Joan XXIII ☎ 93 496 36 00 Ⓜ Maria Cristina, Collblanc

PARTICIPATORY SPORTS

CYCLING

UN COTXE MENYS

Escorted daytime and evening cycle tours around the city.

✉ Carrer Esparteria 3 ☎ 93 268 21 05 Ⓜ Jaume 1

GOLF

EL PRAT GOLF CLUB

This golf club is situated just 15km from Barcelona. You will need to present a membership card of a nationally federated club. Phone or write in advance.

✉ Calle Plans de Bon Vila 17, Terrassa, 08820 El Prat de Llobregat
☎ 93 728 10 00

HORSE RIDING

HIPICA SEVERINO DE SANT CUGAT

Riding lessons and treks through the countryside around Sant Cugat and the Sierra de Collserola.

✉ Paseo Colado 12, Sant Cugat del Vallès ☎ 93 674 11 40

SAILING

BASE NÀUTICA DE LA MAR BELLA

Friendly sailing school that also rents catamarans and windsurfers by the hour.

✉ Avinguda Litoral in the port Mar Bella ☎ 93 221 04 32
Ciutadella-Villa Olímpica

TENNIS

VALL PARC CLUB

Fourteen open-air tennis courts on Tibidabo. Racquets (not balls) for hire.

✉ Carretera Sant Cugat s/n ☎ 93 212 67 89 A6

WHAT`S ON WHEN

JANUARY

Reis Mags (5–6 Jan): the Three Kings arrive by boat, then tour the city, showering the crowds with sweets.

FEBRUARY

Santa Eulàlia (12–19 Feb): a series of musical events in honour of one of the city's patron saints.
Carnestoltes: one week of pre-Lenten carnival celebrations and costumed processions come to an end on Ash Wednesday with the symbolic burial of a sardine.

MARCH

Sant Medir de Gràcia (3 Mar): procession of traditionally dressed horsemen from Gràcia who ride over Collserola to the Hermitage of Sant Medir (Saint of Broad Beans) for a bean-feast.

MARCH/APRIL

Setmana Santa: religious services and celebrations for Easter Week include a solemn procession from the church of Sant

Augustì on Good Friday. Easter celebrations are particularly important in the areas of the city settled by Spaniards from Andalucia and southern Spain.

APRIL

Sant Jordi (23 Apr); the Catalan alternative to St Valentine's Day.

MAY

Festa de la Bicicleta (one Sun in May): join the Mayor and 15,000 others on a cycle-ride around the city, in an effort to encourage fewer cars.

JUNE

Midsummer (23–24 Jun) is a good excuse for huge-scale partying and spectacular fireworks.
Trobada Castellera (mid-June): displays of human-tower building.
International Film Festival (last two weeks)
Flamenco Festival (last two weeks).
Festival del Grec; arts festival (end Jun–Aug).

JULY

Aplec de la Sardana, Olot; the biggest *sardana* dancing festival in Catalonia.

AUGUST

Festa Major de Gràcia (3rd week of Aug): a popular festival of music, dancing and street celebrations in the Gràcia district (➤ 71).

SEPTEMBER

Diada de Catalunya (11 Sep): Catalonia's National Day does not mark a victory, but the taking of the city by Felipe V in 1714.

La Mercè (20–24 Sep): boisterous parades and spectacles featuring giants, devils, dragons, big heads and musically choreographed fireworks.

Festa Major de la Barceloneta (1–15 Oct): one of the liveliest district *festes*, with processions and dancing on the beach every night.

OCTOBER

International Jazz Festival.

DECEMBER

Christmas festivities include a craft fair outside the cathedral (6–23 Dec) and a crib in Plaça Sant Jaume.

Language Guide

In Barcelona there are two official languages, Catalan and Spanish, both coming from Latin but both sounding quite different. Everybody can speak Spanish, although Catalan is most commonly spoken. At most tourist attractions you will always find someone who speaks English, and many restaurants have polyglot menus. However, it is advisable to try to learn at least some Catalan, since English is not as widely spoken as in other European countries. Here is a basic vocabulary to help you with the most essential words and expressions.

hotel	**hotel**	chambermaid	**cambrera**
bed and breakfast	**llit i berenar**	bath	**bany**
single room	**habitació senzilla**	shower	**dutxa**
double room	**habitació doble**	washbasin	**lavabo**
one person	**una persona**	toilet	**toaleta**
one night	**una nit**	balcony	**balcó**
reservation	**reservas**	key	**clau**
room service	**servei d'habitació**	lift	**ascensor**

bank	**banc**	exchange rate	**tant per cent**
exchange office	**oficina de canvi**	commission	**comissió**
post office	**correos**	cashier	**caixer**
coin	**moneda**	change	**camvi**
banknote	**bitllet de banc**	foreign currency	**moneda estrangera**
traveller's cheque	**xec de viatage**	open	**obert**
credit card	**carta de crèdit**	closed	**tancat**

café	**cafè**	starter	**primer plat**
pub/bar	**celler**	main course	**segón plat**
breakfast	**berenar**	dessert	**postres**
lunch	**dinar**	bill	**cuenta**
dinner	**sopar**	beer	**cervesa**
table	**mesa**	wine	**vi**
waiter	**cambrer**	water	**aigua**
waitress	**cambrera**	coffee	**café**

aeroplane	**avió**
airport	**aeroport**
train	**tren**
bus	**autobús**
station	**estació**
boat	**vaixell**
port	**port**
ticket	**bitllet**
single ticket	**senzill-a**
return ticket	**anar i tornar**
non-smoking	**no fumar**
car	**cotxe**
petrol	**gasolina**
bus stop	**la parada**
how do I get to...?	**per anar a...?**

yes	**si**
no	**no**
please	**per favor**
thank you	**gràcies**
hello	**hola**
goodbye	**adéu**
good morning	**bon dia**
good afternoon	**bona tarda**
goodnight	**bona nit**
today	**avui**
tomorrow	**demà**
excuse me	**perdoni**
you're welcome	**de res**
how are you?	**com va?**
do you speak English?	**parla anglès?**
I don't understand	**no ho enten**
how much?	**quant es?**
where is...?	**on és...?**

Practicalities

WHAT YOU NEED

● Required
○ Suggested
▲ Not required

Some countries require a passport to remain valid for a minimum period (usually at least six months) beyond the date of entry – contact their consulate or embassy or your travel agent for details.

	UK	Germany	USA	Netherlands	Spain
Passport/National Identity Card	●	●	●	●	●
Visa (regulations can change – check before your journey)	▲	▲	▲	▲	▲
Onward or Return Ticket	▲	▲	▲	▲	▲
Health Inoculations	▲	▲	▲	▲	▲
Health Documentation (reciprocal agreement document) (➤ 248, Health)	●	●	●	●	●
Travel Insurance	○	○	○	○	○
Driving Licence (national – EU format/national/Spanish trnsltn/interntnal)	●	●	●	●	●
Car Insurance Certificate (if own car)	●	●	●	●	●
Car Registration Document (if own car)	●	●	●	●	●

TOURIST OFFICES

In the UK
Spanish Tourist Office
79 New Cavendish Street
London W1W 6XB
☎ (020) 7486 8077
Fax: (020) 7486 8034
www.spain.info

In the USA
Tourist Office of Spain
666 Fifth Avenue (35th floor)
New York
NY 10103
☎ (1212) 265-8822
Fax: (1212) 265-8864

Tourist Office of Spain
8383 Wilshire Boulevard
Suite 960
Beverley Hills
CA 90211
☎ (1213) 658-7192
Fax: (1213) 658-1061

CUSTOMS

YES

From another EU country for personal use (guidelines)

800 cigarettes, 200 cigars,
1 kilogram of tobacco
10 litres of spirits (over 22%)
20 litres of aperitifs
90 litres of wine, of which 60 litres can be sparkling wine
110 litres of beer

From a non-EU country for your personal use, the allowances are:

200 cigarettes OR
50 cigars OR 250 grams of tobacco
1 litre of spirits (over 22%)
2 litres of intermediary products (eg sherry) and sparkling wine
2 litres of still wine
50 grams of perfume
0.25 litres of eau de toilette
The value limit for goods is 175 euros

Travellers under 17 years of age are not entitled to the tobacco and alcohol allowances.

NO

Drugs, firearms, ammunition, offensive weapons, obscene material, unlicensed animals.

WHEN TO GO

Average figures for Barcelona

High season

Low season

	JAN	FEB	MAR	APR	MAY	JUN	JUL	AUG	SEP	OCT	NOV	DEC
Season	Low	Low	Low	High	High	High	High	High	High	Low	Low	Low
Temperature	16°C	17°C	18°C	21°C	23°C	27°C	29°C	29°C	27°C	23°C	19°C	17°C
Weather	Cloud	Cloud	Wet	Cloud	Sun	Sun	Sun	Sun	Sunshine & showers	Wet	Wet	Sunshine & showers

Very wet Wet Cloud Sun Sunshine & showers

ARRIVING

Spain's national airline, Iberia, has scheduled flights to Barcelona's El Prat de Llobregat Airport from major Spanish and European cities. The city is served by over 30 international airlines including BA, Delta, KLM, Lufthansa and Virgin Express.

El Prat de Llobregat Airport

12km to city centre

Journey times

- Train: 20 minutes
- Bus: 40 minutes
- Car: 30 minutes

Estacio de França Railway Station

Near city centre

Near Barceloneta

Journey times

- Train: available
- Bus: available
- Car: available

MONEY

The euro is the official currency of Spain.

Banknotes are in denominations of 5, 10, 20, 50, 100, 200 and 500 euros; coins are in denominations of 1, 2, 5, 10, 20 and 50 cents, and 1 and 2 euros.

Euro traveller's cheques are widely accepted, as are major credit cards. Credit and debit cards can also be used for withdrawing euro notes from ATMs.

€10

€50

€100

€200

TIME

Like the rest of Spain, Catalonia is one hour ahead of Greenwich Mean Time (GMT+1), except from late March to late October, when summer time (GMT+2) operates.

TOURIST OFFICES

Turisme de Barcelona
www.barcelonaturisme.com
Plaça de Catalunya 17
☎ 93 368 97 30
Daily 9–9

The main tourist office is situated beneath Plaça de Catalunya. Services include hotel reservations, currency exchange, walking tours and theatre and concert tickets.

There are branches of the city tourist office on the ground floor of the city hall and at the Sants railway station.

Plaça Sant Jaume I
Mon–Sat 10–8, Sun 10–2
Sants Railway Station (Estació de Sants)
Mon–Fri 8–8, Sat–Sun 8–2

There are also tourist information offices in the airport arrival halls, open daily 9–9.

Turisme de Catalunya
Palau Robert
Passeig de Gràcia 105
☎ 93 238 40 00
Mon–Sat 10–7, Sun 10–2

In summer, information booths can be found at Sagrada Família and La Rambla. In the Barrí Gòtic, you may also come across uniformed tourist officials, known as 'Red Jackets'.

NATIONAL HOLIDAYS

JAN	FEB	MAR	APR	MAY	JUN	JUL	AUG	SEP	OCT	NOV	DEC
2	0	1(2)	(2)	(1)1	(1)1	0	1	2	1	1	4

1 Jan	New Year's Day
6 Jan	Three Kings
19 Mar	Sant Josep
Mar/Apr	Good Friday, Easter Monday
1 May	Labour Day
May/Jun	Whit Monday
24 Jun	St John
15 Aug	Assumption
11 Sep	Catalan National Day
24 Sep	Our Lady of Mercy
12 Oct	Hispanitat
1 Nov	All Saints' Day
6 Dec	Constitution Day
8 Dec	Feast of teh Immaculate Conception
25 Dec	Christmas Day
26 Dec	Sant Esteve

OPENING HOURS

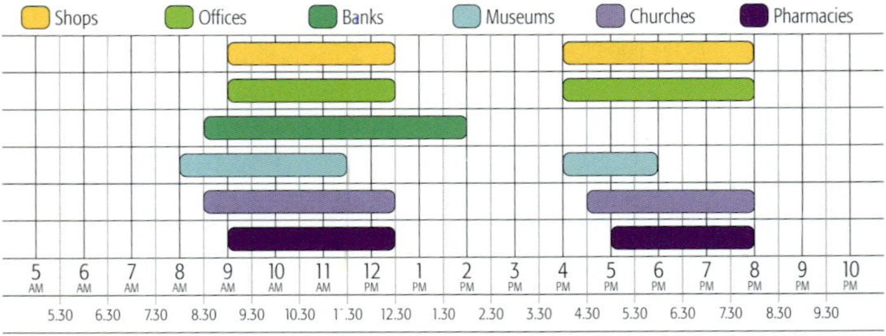

Large department stores and supermarkets may open outside these times, especially in summer. Business hours also vary depending on the season, with many companies working *horas intensivas* in summer, from 8–3. Banks generally close on Saturdays, although some main branches open in the morning 8.30–12.30. Outside banking hours, money-exchange facilities are available at the airport and Sants railway station. Some *barris* (districts) also have their own separate feast days, when some shops and offices may close.

PERSONAL SAFETY

The Policía Municipal (navy-blue uniforms) keep law and order in the city. For a police station ask for la comisaría.

To help prevent crime:

- Do not carry more cash than you need
- Beware of pickpockets in markets, tourist sights or crowded places
- Avoid walking alone in dark alleys at night, especially in the Barri Xines.
- Leave valuables and important documents in the hotel or apartment safe.

City Police assistance:
☎ 092 from any call box

PUBLIC TRANSPORT

Metro The metro is the easiest and fastest way of moving around the city. There are two different underground train systems, the Metro with its five lines identified by number and colour, and the FGC (☎ 93 205 15 15) with two lines in Barcelona and four more lines going to nearby towns.

Buses Barcelona has an excellent bus network; pick up a free plan from any tourist office. Timetables are also shown at individual bus stops. Buses run 5:30am–11pm. At night there is a Nitbus with routes centred on Plaça de Catalunya. Throughout the year the Bus Turístic, a hop-on-hop-off service, circuits the main city sights.

Trains The Spanish railway system, RENFE, runs trains from Barcelona to all the major cities in Spain and some outside. Many main-line trains stop at the underground stations at Passeig de Gràcia and Plaça de Catalunya. There are two main railway stations: Estació de Sants and Estació de França near Barceloneta.

Boat Trips The best way to admire the port and coastline is from the sea. Golondrinas offer frequent 35-minute harbour tours or 2-hour voyages to the Port Olímpic (➤ 45). Although Barcelona is the biggest port in the Mediterranean, the only regular passenger services are to the Balearic islands.

Cable cars, Funiculars and the Tramvia Blau A cable car connects the lower city with Montjuïc castle and links with the funicular railway. To reach Tibidabo, take the Tramvia Blau (Blue Tram), then the Funicular del Tibidabo to the Amusement Park at the top of the hill.

DRIVING

Speed limit on motorways (*autopistas*): **120kph**

Speed limit on main roads : **100kph**

On minor roads: **90kph**

Speed limit in towns (*Poblaciones*): **50kph**

Seat belts must be worn in front seats at all times and in rear seats where fitted.

Random breath-testing. Never drive under the influence of alcohol.

Fuel (*gasolina*) is available as: *Super Plus* (98 octane), *Super* (96 octane), unleaded or *sin plomo* (90 octane) and *gasoleo* or *gasoil* (diesel). Petrol stations are normally open 6am–10pm, and closed Sundays, though larger ones are open 24 hours. Most take credit cards.

If you break down driving your own car and are a member of an AIT-affiliated motoring club, you can call the Real Automóvil Club de Catalunya (☎ 93 228 50 00). If the car is hired, follow the instructions given in the documentation; most of the international rental firms provide a rescue service.

CAR RENTAL

The leading international car rental companies have offices at Barcelona airport and you can book a car in advance (essential in peak periods) either direct or through a travel agent. Local companies offer competitive rates and will usually deliver a car to the airport.

TELEPHONES

Phonecards (*credifone*) are available from post offices and tobacconists (*estancs*) for €6.01 or €12.02.

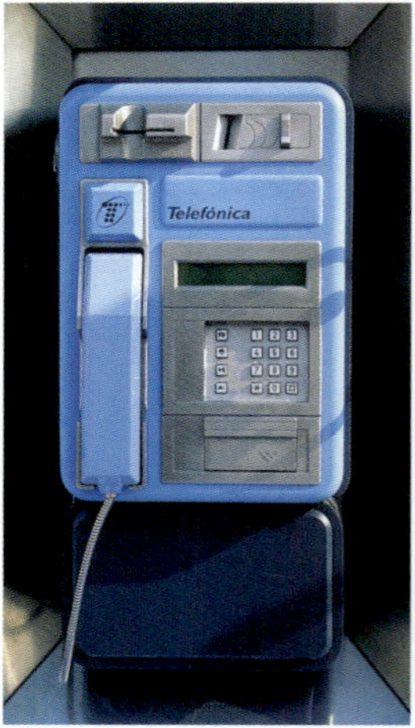

International Dialling Codes

From Spain to:

UK: 00 44
USA & Canada: 00 1
France: 00 33
Germany: 00 49
Netherlands: 00 31

Reduced prices apply to calls made between 10pm and 8am and on Saturdays after 2pm.

POST

Post Offices

Most post offices (*correos*) open Mon–Fri, 8:30–2 but some also open in the afternoon and on Saturday morning. The main post office (*Oficina Central*) at Via Laietana 1 is open Mon–Sat 8:30am–9pm, Sun 8am–2pm, and the Eixample post office at Carrer Aragó 282 is open Mon–Fri 8am–9pm and Sat 9–2. You can also buy stamps at any tobacconist (*estanc*).

TIPS/GRATUITIES

Yes ✓ No ✗

Restaurants (if service not included)	✓	10%
Cafés/bars (if service not included)	✓	change
Taxis	✓	10%
Tour guides	✓	€1
Porters	✓	€1
Chambermaids	✓	€1
Hairdressers	✓	change
Cloakroom attendants	✓	change
Theatre/cinema usherettes	✓	change
Toilets	✗	

HEALTH

Insurance Nationals of EU and certain other countries can get medical treatment in Spain with the relevant documentation (Form E111 for Britons), although private medical insurance is still advised and is essential for all other visitors.

Dental Services Dental treatment is not usually available free of charge as all dentists practise privately. A list of *dentistas* can be found in the yellow pages of the telephone directory. Dental treatment should be covered by private medical insurance.

Sun Advice The sunniest (and hottest) months are July and August, with an average of 11 hours sun a day and daytime temperatures of 29°C. Particularly during these months you should avoid the midday sun and use a strong sunblock.

Drugs Prescription and non-prescription drugs and medicines are available from pharmacies (*farmàcias*), distinguished by a large green cross. They are able to dispense many drugs that would be available only on prescription in other countries.

Safe Water Tap water is generally safe though it can be heavily chlorinated. Mineral water is cheap to buy and is sold as *con gaz* (carbonated) and *sin gaz* (still). Drink plenty of water during hot weather.

ELECTRICITY

The power supply is usually 220 volts but a few old buildings are still wired for 125 volts. Sockets accept two-round-pin-style plugs, so an adaptor is needed for most non-Continental appliances and a transformer for appliances operating on 110–120 volts.

TAXIS

Pick up a black and yellow taxi at a taxi rank or hail one if it's displaying a green light and the sign *Lliure/Libre* (free). Fares are not unduly expensive but extra fees are charged for airport trips and for baggage. Prices are shown on a sticker inside.

CONCESSIONS

Students Holders of an International Student Identity Card (ISIC) may be able to obtain some concessions on travel, entrance fees etc. Most museums offer 50 per cent discount to students, and many are free on the first Sunday of each month. There are several IYHF youth hostels in the city, with accommodation in multi-bed dormitories. Expect to pay around €6–10 per person.

Senior Citizens Barcelona is a popular destination for older travellers, especially during winter. Most museums and galleries offer a 50 per cent discount for retired people.

Index

ACKNOWLEDGEMENTS

The Automobile Association would like to thank the following photo libraries for their assistance in the preparation of this book.

Brand X Pics 218; **Corbis UK** 226; **DigitalVision** 220, 223; **Photodisc** 147, 239.

The remaining photographs are held in the Automobile Association's own Photo Library (AA World Travel Library) and were taken by the following photographers:

Michelle Chaplow 10/1, 13, 16, 20, 27, 28/9, 44, 47, 64, 80, 110, 111, 159, 166, 170/1, 191, 200, 206, 208, 211, 217, 230, 232, 246, 247, 254/5; **Steve Day** front cover, 1, 2t, 2bl, 19, 21, 22/3, 23, 31, 32, 38/9, 50/1, 53, 54, 61, 67, 69, 88, 90/1, 97, 101, 104/5, 106/7, 109, 112, 114/5, 117, 118, 122/3, 127; **Philip Enticknap** 102, 169, 174, 178/9, 180, 183, 186/7, 189; **Max Jourdan** 2/3, 14/5, 24, 36/7, 45, 48/9, 62, 63, 70, 72, 76, 82/3, 86/7, 94, 124, 134/5, 136, 139, 154, 214, 243; **Simon McBride** 75, 93, 128/9, 130, 133, 143, 149, 150, 152/3, 192, 198/9, 203, 205, 213; **Peter Wilson** 30, 34, 42/3, 77, 98, 119, 120, 162/3, 173.

Typesetting: **Information Engineers** Page layout: **Pentacor book design**
Editors: **Marilynne Lanng, Pam Stagg** Design support: **Katherine Mead**